A BANNER HANDBOOK FOR HOMESCHOOLERS

Elinor Miller

iUniverse, Inc.
New York   Bloomington

A BANNER HANDBOOK FOR HOMESCHOOLERS

Copyright © 2009 Elinor Miller

All rights reserved. No part of this book may be used or reproduced by any means,
graphic, electronic, or mechanical, including photocopying, recording, taping or by
any information storage retrieval system without the written permission of the publisher
except in the case of brief quotations embodied in critical articles and reviews.

iUniverse books may be ordered through booksellers or by contacting:

iUniverse
1663 Liberty Drive
Bloomington, IN 47403
www.iuniverse.com
1-800-Authors (1-800-288-4677)

Because of the dynamic nature of the Internet, any Web addresses or links contained in this
book may have changed since publication and may no longer be valid. The views expressed in
this work are solely those of the author and do not necessarily reflect the views of the publisher,
and the publisher hereby disclaims any responsibility for them.

ISBN: 978-1-4401-5323-5 (pbk)
ISBN: 978-1-4401-5324-2 (ebook)

Printed in the United States of America

iUniverse rev. date: 9/18/09

"Then shall the eyes of the blind be op'd
And the ears of the deaf unstopped"
Isaiah 35:5

Probe and Shed Light

Contents

ACKNOWLEDGEMENTS

A. Donna Ogle, a leading educator of the National Urban Alliance (http://www. nuatc.org/), has been a devoted supporter of Word Web Vocabulary for many years. She sends her teacher-students at trade shows to Word Web's booth, and many classroom teachers now use Word Web because she gave them the word to do so.

B. Many thanks to Susan Hyde, college English instructor, freelance writer, and homeschooling parent for her positive assessment of Word Web Vocabulary: http://packaged-curricula.suite101.com/article.cfm/word_web_vocabulary_review

C. Many of my friends and family were quite skeptical when I told them I would be enrolling our son in The Banner School for its first year. How did I know it would even be a good school?

What we got was small classes and, surprise, an **integrated curriculum**! I was gratified to find that Mrs. Miller's take on a complete education was that the subjects not be taught in isolation. I distinctly remember the year when the entire school focused on Egypt. Egyptian art in art class, students in math class using hieroglyphic notations, vocabulary words from the period being used in terrific sentences, and so on.

The other example that jumps into my head is the year of the insects. Careful drawings in art class led to a visit to the insect zoo at the Smithsonian. I would have loved to have been the proverbial "fly on the wall" when the curators heard even some first graders discussing the differences between lepidoptera and hymenoptera (which of course had been some of the whole-school vocabulary words). What was amazing was that students from first grade on were ALL learning this material. And they were excited to be learning it!

Even now, some twenty-five years later (and with 17 years teaching in a local public school system under my belt), I still hold up Mrs. Miller's immersion ideas as an educational ideal."   *Jacqueline M. Callis*

D. "Elinor Miller is an amazing educator with innovative teaching ideas. Her vocabulary program is quite motivating for students and is altogether enjoyable for both the teacher and students. Another great teaching method is her integration of subjects - she would choose a social studies topic (like the Middle Ages or ancient Greece), and then in addition to teaching the history, the lessons would encompass math, language arts, music, art, and science. The students learned an impressive amount of material. After Elinor founded The Banner School in Frederick, Maryland, the school grew quickly because of her expertise and creativity."

Susan Haines
Reading Specialist
Montgomery County (MD) Public Schools
Gaithersburg, Maryland

FOREWORD:
My Philosophical Support
for Homeschooling

"Although public schools do teach facts," as Cal Thomas states, *"when students study American History, math, grammar, other cultures, there's a lot more to teaching than just the facts. Facts, however, can be a 'turn-off' for many students. It's how they are presented that makes the difference between apathy and excitement."*

This third "Banner" book enables me to share the materials and techniques I created when teaching before and after founding The Banner School. I particularly value those times when I discovered the right methods that helped children overcome their apathy or found the best approach to help those with learning problems.

I include original ideas and methods for instruction that didn't fit my previous books with the expectation that these will enrich your children's education and will counter the effects on those who may be part of the "wired generation" caught up in texting, use of cell phones, iPods, and other devices. I hope I am not "too out of it" to get tweens and teens to take an interest in the variety of activities I explain below.

I trust that homeschooling parents will direct their children's interests toward wholesome practices that involve those I feel are beneficial for them. I champion those who teach their children at home or in a special school where they can choose the subjects and curricular materials. I hope the insights I present in this book will prove helpful and inspiring to many families. I believe that much of my material will prove to be effective with children of varying ages, abilities, and interests.

I am especially pleased to be able to share these unusual projects I have created especially for home-learning children: "101 Ways to Approach a Writing Assignment"; CommuniCards'; guidance and substance for interdisciplinary science and social studies topics; unusual and diverse math strategies; vocabulary and language lessons; a stormy-day home pursuit; The Big Sit', a one-of-a-kind field trip; a fresh approach to students' study of Joyce Kilmer's "Trees;" and my persistent encouragement for students to focus on our visual world.

Despite having bypassed the standard route to become a teacher, the extremely positive feedback I receive from other teachers reassures me that I understand how to provide sound educational material to a span of ages. The gratefulness of Banner School's parents for the blossoming of their children contributes another source of confidence in my abilities. It might interest readers to learn that during the ten years at which I headed Banner, few of those teachers had a teaching certificate. They were "natural-born teachers," ones with intuition about how to meet children's needs, diagnose problems, instruct, and intent on learning new methods and techniques.

I hope I will hear from many parents/children who will describe positive experiences that arose from using this book. I expect most of my material to have "fun" written all over it, because with few exceptions, learning is fun!

PREFACE:
Kindling a Teaching Passion

*"The real voyage of discovery consists not in seeking
new landscapes but in having new eyes."*
Marcel Proust

My first two years of schooling at a small private school where we had spelling bees, learned French, improved penmanship by copying common sayings, and were surrounded in the lunchroom by historic scenes may have influenced my outlook on how to educate children.

I graduated from college with a Bachelor's degree in social anthropology, met my husband, married, had three children, and settled for ten years in western Massachusetts where I began my teaching career. Despite having tutored students in algebra and geometry for many years, I never thought of myself as a teacher. However, I decided to act on the public schools' desperate need for substitutes.

Perhaps my credentials are not what one expects from a long-term middle-school teacher, to say nothing of one who founded an elementary and middle school, since my training as a teacher was accomplished "on-the-job." Although my college pedagogy was unrelated to any field of education, my BA degree opened public schools' doors for me. Whether that would be true today, I do not know, but in the sixties, it was. I drew my inspiration not from theorists but from my own experiences.

I taught many math classes and also filled in for classroom teachers. I used the at-hand instructional material, some of which I liked, while others I didn't. I was distressed when lesson plans called for me to move on when I felt students weren't ready. Although I didn't know it then, I had begun to develop my philosophy of education. Later, when I had my own classrooms, I was still required to use the schools' materials and follow a specific schedule.

Probe and Shed Light

However, after moving to Parkersburg, West Virginia, I taught middle school math and English classes in a K-12 private school. I no longer had to follow others' plan books or regimented schedules but could create my own ... AND the principal ordered texts that I requested! During my years at this academy, I grew in the art of teaching. I enjoyed finding ways to succeed with students who varied in their academic abilities and their modes of learning, as well as a few indifferent students. I questioned the use of standard report cards which I didn't feel gave parents enough details about their children's performance or ease of learning. This caused an entry into my growing "If- only-I-had- a-school-of-my-own, I'd ..." notebook!

My years of tutoring math afforded me many insights into the bases for students' errors, while my in-the-classroom training presented me with frequent opportunities to work with students from diverse backgrounds. Even private schools— or, perhaps, especially private schools — enroll children with distinctly different educational experiences, types of knowledge, abilities, disparate home environments, and often no familiarity with English.

Looking back to my own high school days also brought me a new type of understanding which I wish was more widespread. I had excelled year after year in math, so much so that my seventh grade teacher directed me tutor my classmates, and I was in every high school honors class except English. This latter circumstance disturbed me quite a bit, but I just didn't "get" nouns, verbs, and other parts of speech, nor could I diagram sentences. I also disliked analyzing literature, although at home I was an avid reader. Such anomalies are hard to explain, especially when someone like me ends up becoming an English teacher— when, finally, I <u>did</u> understand all that had baffled me before!

During my years at the helm of a classroom, I developed the philosophy that few students are capable (or desirous) of learning all that others expect of them. I accepted the fact that just as most people have varying ways of learning, an equal number of paths exist to direct them toward success. I became aware that what works for one student may not work for another, but like all teachers, I did my best to provide each student with the elements that would produce an educated individual with the necessary skills to make his way in the world. I also learned that a child's classroom performance might bear little relevance to what his future held.

This insight was reinforced when I attended my 40th high school reunion. I was surprised to discover that some of those in my graduating class who'd been mostly in remedial classes had gone on to become principals of schools and successful entrepreneurs! I have gotten news of a number of former Banner students who had struggled with their daily assignments but are doing just fine today in the "real world."

One challenge I particularly remember was the year when two girls arrived in my seventh grade class, neither of whom could read or write, yet in conversation both were quite bright. Not knowing how to work with them, I enrolled in West Virginia University's graduate program in Parkersburg. The class I chose was diagnosing learning disabilities, where I absorbed the research which explained how we learn to read and write—or don't. I became certified to administer specific tests that would identify these girls' problems. The results enabled me to apply techniques to help them with their disabilities and to give their parents direction.

These outcomes encouraged me to obtain a M.Ed. degree so that I could acquire the necessary know-how to diagnose and remediate future students with learning difficulties. Later, this advanced degree gave me credibility when I founded The Banner School.

The more I learned about the various reasons that could impede a student's learning, the more I desired to devise different approaches that would circumvent these. In other words, I looked for different techniques to achieve specific goals.

In 1982 I was finally able to put my foot where my mouth had been for many years. Soon after my husband and I moved to Frederick, MD, we bought a building in the heart of the city, renovated it, and named it The Banner School. *A Banner Experience,* details its founding and how it grew over the next ten years from the original 24 students in grades 1-5, to several hundred in kindergarten through eighth grade on three campuses.

In 1992, when we were finally all together on one site, I decided to retire. My ideas on educating children, especially through the use of a structured vocabulary program and a significant reference pool for science and social studies, were well entrenched by that time, and I no longer felt challenged to continue at the school's helm.

I look forward to sharing the materials I have created with the hope that you will put many of them into practice.

CHAPTER I

▼

THE ART OF PARENTING

I share my insights into some of the common issues parents face and offer guidance garnered from my thirty years of classroom teaching and as Head of The Banner School. I hope you will benefit from my insights whether you are teaching your own children or they are learning elsewhere and that you will share them with friends who might benefit from my thoughts.

Furthermore, I have decided to declare a ban on kids! Not living, breathing, laughing kids, but the prevalent use of this word. Where did children, youngsters, grade schoolers, siblings, teens, moppets, and tots go? Almost every reference in magazines and online links to information I promote in this book use "kids" in their titles.

I. THE ACCEPTING PARENT

When our children are very young, we are constantly proud of them. We show off their pictures taken in the nursery. We describe each new development: The first tooth, the first step, the first word and so on. We beam. We flash pictures. Right from the start we feel we have the perfect child.

Parents show how proud they are of their children when they give birthday parties for them, plan purchases of new clothes and take them on interesting outings. However, as children grow older, it is not always as easy to show pride in them, especially if they do not get good grades in school, make an athletic team, or win awards for other endeavors. Not all children make A's in school or achieve in a conspicuous fashion. In fact, many will have problems that impede their learning or prevent them from participating in athletic or after-school programs.

The truth of the matter is that most of our children, regardless of the amount of love we lavish on them and the careful nurturing they receive, will not turn out

Probe and Shed Light

to be super achievers. Many of them are going to be ordinary—just like most of us. And yet, each child has many traits that are easy to admire, and parents must remember to appreciate these. Coaches try to teach their team members that it's not the winning that is important; it's how well the team plays. Parents should do the same.

Over a period of years I saw a great number of children come and go through my classrooms. I watched many progress from kindergarten into adulthood, and I realize how blessed are the children who grow up to be everything their parents want them to be. Even more so are the ones whose parents never expect them to fulfill a set agenda of careers and lifestyles.

Parents who accept, respect, and value their children for their uniqueness are likely to rear coping and confidant children. Parents who judge and are constantly disapproving of their children's choices and tastes deny them the support they should provide. Parents need not be overly permissive in order to show this support.

Since homeschooling parents have such a close association with their children, I think it likely that they shoulder the responsibility for teaching their children good table manners and other elements of etiquette, guide them in their decision making, and do not allow them to make negative and derisive comments about others' hobbies and interests, or their prowess—or lack thereof—in sports, graphic arts, and music.

Here are some do's and don'ts for the accepting parent:

Do: Look for talents your children possess and support them in as many ways as possible. If one is intensely interested in a subject, do all you can to encourage him. Take him to the library so he can get relevant materials; provide him with lessons if that is appropriate; take him to museums or shows that fit his interest; talk to him about it, attend any functions in which he is a part.

Don't: Decide your children's careers. Make sure you give them plenty of natural exposure to the vocations you would like them to choose but do it in a way that doesn't suggest their need to comply. If you'd like your off-springs to take over the family business, see that they have frequent opportunities to visit your office, and as they become teens that they have Saturday and summer jobs there. Just don't talk to them in terms of their becoming a permanent part of the operation until they give you some indication that that is what they would like to do.

Do: Treat your grown children as you would other adults. Ask their opinions on politics, money matters, hair-styles, just the way you discuss subjects with your contemporaries.

Don't: Offer advice unless it is sought.

And remember this age-old advice: If you have nothing good to say, say nothing at all. Your rewards as an accepting parent will be many, but the most important will be your knowing that you have raised your children to be confident, coping people, who, in turn, will probably become accepting parents themselves.

II. HELP YOUR CHILD GAIN SELF-CONFIDENCE

My mother taught me very early to believe I could achieve any accomplishment
I wanted to. The first was to walk without braces.
Wilma Rudolph

Often a child will work hard to win—to be a success—because this earns praise, but he may totally miss the enjoyment and satisfaction that come simply from taking part. If he doesn't reach his goal—or the goal his parents have set for him—he may lose confidence in himself. He may become afraid of failure. Love and family values can do much to reduce this fear. With competition all around us, children see how we idolize "winning" in our work, our sports, our lives. No wonder it rubs off on them!

"My dad's better than your dad because he drives a Mercedes."

"My team's better than your team because we won the championship."

"I beat you because I got 94% on the test and you only got 85."

Consider the following points when helping your youngsters develop pride in themselves and confidence in their abilities:

1. Success in sports isn't as important as getting involved and enjoying it. Both children and adults have trouble with this idea. Eight-year-olds, for example, should play hockey or soccer for fun, not championships. Similarly, to expect a girl who is a poor swimmer to "come home with a medal" is also unfair. Let her swim for fun. The rewards: Learning teamwork and cooperation, developing skills, testing limits. The goal is not to win every time. Self-confidence comes with meeting challenges—big ones and small ones.

   Too often, we cheer the champ and ignore the loser. We all know about "Soccer Moms" and "Hockey Dads." More cooperation among parents, coaches, teachers, and youth leaders could do much to reduce the importance of winning and help to build self-confidence. The key question after the game should not be, "Did you win?" but "Did you have fun?"

2. Children need academic goals that match ambition to ability. To ask an average student to be satisfied with nothing less than a B in every subject is putting too much stress on success. Every child has one or two subjects that he understands or enjoys more than the rest. Praise these and encourage the others

3. Children need positive rather than sarcastic comments. If your child has a poor game or a low grade on a test, don't greet him with: "Well, you sure blew it today!" Try encouragement instead. When he's discouraged—"I'm really lousy"—let him express his feelings but help him to see himself in a better light. Point out past achievements. Remind him of his special skills. Share this outlook of Theodore Roosevelt: *"I care not what others think of what I do, but I care very much about what I think of what I do. That is character!"*

4. Children must know that your love is NOT linked to their accomplishments. Confidence blossoms in a home that is full of love and affection. Love, security and acceptance are at the heart of family life. Triumphs and defeats should be expected and accepted.

In your role as parent, there are many ways to help your child see that he can perform well, earn recognition, and develop a sense of accomplishment:

1. Assign household chores such as tidying a room, washing the car, or doing something else that comes easily; be sure to give the necessary recognition when the task is satisfactorily completed. Increase your child's responsibilities as soon as you are sure he is ready.

2. Use family games and neighborhood sports. The whole family should try to participate, but don't "let" her win. Your little deception may only add to her feeling of failure. ("I'm so bad that Dad thinks he has to let me win.") A handicap system is a good way to balance skills.

3. Don't hide your own failures. Were you hopeless in math? Did you once score a crucial goal against your own team? It helps a youngster to see that Mummy and Daddy weren't perfect either, yet they turned out okay.

4. Encourage less achievement and more light-hearted enjoyment. We don't have to be good at something to enjoy it.

    Remember that for every winner there are many who don't win. A child's confidence in himself doesn't come from winning. It comes from a solid foundation of family love. It comes from coping with problems and mastering them. You can make the difference.

*"The principle is competing against yourself. It's about self improvement,
about being better than you were the day before."*
Steve Young

III. HOW TELEVISION AFFECTS MINDS AND BODIES

As an educator, I am delighted whenever I hear parents and legislators express heightened anxiety about the effects of television on children. Teachers and school administrators have long decried the negative influences it has on students' minds, but it is only now after many acts of children's violence and destruction have received front-page status, that there is a general outcry by many to see more supervision and restrictions placed on the contents of television programs and video games.

Television has been described as "the raucous life of the party that won't leave the house." According to the A.C. Nielsen Company, this omnipresent beast is on an average of seven hours and 38 minutes a day in American households. This means that from birth on, children are surrounded by sensory stimulants. They become accustomed to an environment filled with noise, and they grow accustomed to focusing on constantly changing visual patterns. Teachers and child psychologists today see ever more children with hyperactivity and attention deficit disorder. Could it be that mega-doses of television are responsible?

Jane Healy, author of *Endangered Minds*, says, "Children heavily exposed to the 'whole video culture' often are disadvantaged when they reach school age. They have learned a visual, fast-paced, unconnected, thoughtless type of approach to problem solving. Many children diagnosed as learning disabled do not have anything wrong with their brains; they just process information differently. The brain that is fed a steady diet of video games is different from the brain that has read, been read to, and spent time talking and playing quietly." Teachers report that young people of the television generation have no patience for study in depth; they want quick, simple, unambiguous answers.

Dr. Neil Postman, professor at New York University and author of *The Disappearance of Childhood*, claims television is turning out to be "a disastrous influence on the way children learn." He finds that television appears to be shortening the attention span of the young, as well as eroding, to a considerable extent, their linguistic powers and their ability to handle mathematical symbolism.

In fact, the more a student watches TV, the worse his performance in school. The 6th and 12th grade students who took part in a survey of more than 500,000

California public school students showed a decline in reading, language and arithmetic scores for each hour of television watched per day, <u>no matter how much homework they did, how intelligent there were, or how much money their parents earned.</u>

In another type of study, findings have recently come to light that provide evidence that spending too many hours sitting in front of the "tube" may contribute to the obesity that now afflicts more American children than ever and that excessive TV watching also appears to go hand in hand with high blood cholesterol levels.

Researchers at the University of California, Irvine, matched more than 1,000 young children's and adolescents' cholesterol measurements with their TV-viewing habits and found that those who reported watching at least two hours of television a day were twice as likely to have high blood cholesterol - above 200 milligrams per deciliter of blood - as those who tuned into television for less than two hours daily. Children who watched four or more hours a day were nearly four times as likely to end up with cholesterol levels over 200.

Be sure to read Jane Healey's *Endangered Minds*:
http://www.newhorizons.org/future/Creating_the_Future/crfut_healy.html?

MORE TRUTHS ABOUT TELEVISION

- By the time children are 5 years old, many have watched television for as many hours as it takes to earn an undergraduate degree. Margery Kraynik, *Starting School.*
- The worst thing one can do for a hyperactive child is to put him or her in front of a television set. Television activates the child at the same time that it cuts the child off from real sensory stimulation and the opportunity for resolution.
- From ages 6 to 18, the average child watches TV 16,000 to 18,000 hours and attends school about 13,000. Studies show the more TV, the poorer the student does on standard achievement tests.
- A third grader spends an average of 900 hours a year in class—and 1170 hours watching television.
- Teachers report that young people of the television generation have no patience for study in depth; they want quick, simple, unambiguous answers.

Don't we owe it to our children to put a reasonable lid on TV consumption?

IV. HOW TO REAR STRESS-FREE CHILDREN

The joys of parents are secret, and so are their griefs and fears:
They cannot utter the one, nor will they utter the other.
Francis Bacon "Of Parents and Children"

Parents can ensure that childhood is the carefree and happy time they want it to be for their children. Responsible parents can see that stress does not become partners with their children, producing disastrous effects on the way they think and in the way they behave.

Although sources of childhood stress are many, parents play the deciding role in determining whether their child will become an independent, confident, coping person, or one who suffers from the effects of stress: Bedwetting, anger, anxiety, not going to sleep easily at night, crying too easily, aggressiveness, overeating, hair twisting, teeth clenching, biting himself, and withdrawal. Since most stress starts in the home, parents should follow these guidelines.

Provide a home environment that is calm and anti-frantic. Even when both parents work, difficult as it may be, this is necessary for your child's wellbeing. If you're not homeschooling, in the evening, prepare clothes, books, papers, and lunch together for the next day.

Parents would not believe how extraordinarily stressed elementary school children are when they open their lunch box and find food they do not enjoy. "Why doesn't she remember that I hate tuna/mustard/jelly on my peanut butter?" More often than not, the lunch goes angrily and uneaten into the trash.

See that your child gets the 10 to 11 hours of sleep a night that most professionals agree elementary-age school children need. Teachers comment often on how tired many of their students are and consequently how difficult it is for them to concentrate. Not being able to keep up in class is a sure source of stress.

Get up each day in time for an unhurried and nutritious breakfast. If you send your child off to school with little or no breakfast and a remembrance of frenzied efforts to get everyone out of the house on time, you have set your child up for a bad morning at school. Imagine children having to unwind before they can settle in to their school day!

See that your child is not overscheduled, that he is not involved in after-school activities that total more than 3 to 7 hours a week. Allow opportunities for genuine unstructured and noncompetitive play, nature's way of helping children reduce stress.

Familiarize yourself with the developmental stages through which children go so that you avoid placing your child in stress-producing situations. Read books and/or attend classes on child development to learn what activities are appropriate for a child and when.

For instance, parents who expose their 9-year-old to a PG-13 movie or a 13-year-old to an R-rated one feel it's okay "Because I am there with him." Well, it's **not** okay. Just being there is not enough to overcome the effects of too-mature material. Children cannot deal with subject matter that is not appropriate for them. It stays on their minds and troubles them, even though they shield this from their parents. Believe it or not, more parents that you would think possible use this method as a way to explain "the facts of life."

In a similar vein, do not send your elementary child to school or group meetings with expensive watches, hair clips, and the like. Young children are not ready to take responsibilities for such articles, nor do they value them in the same way that an adult does. I have seen too many angry mothers and too many frightened children when such items turn up missing.

Do not "overparent" or overprotect, or your child will not become a confident, coping person. From the time your child is born, you should have a plan for the long process known as "cutting the apron strings." Be willing to leave your child with a babysitter—even if he is wailing when you depart. If you take your child to school, let him enter the building by himself. If you are overprotective, the message you give is not one of love and support but rather one that says, "You haven't got what it takes; let me help you." As you know, it's not what you say, but what you do that counts.

Expect and encourage your child to take responsibility and pride in what he accomplishes. A 3-year-old can make her own bed. It may be lumpy, but she'll improve the process in a remarkably short time. Don't jump in and help. Children need to struggle with tasks in order to grow and to have a foundation on which to build in the future. In addition, don't sabotage your child's efforts to make decisions—though you feel they are incorrect.

Allow your children to take those steps towards independence for which they indicate they are ready. This does not mean saying "yes" to every request and demand, but it does mean thinking over carefully your negative responses. Is there any true reason why Susie can't wait unattended at the school bus stop? Why isn't it all right for Sam to ride his bicycle further than your residential street? Why can't John walk to school by himself? These may be valid desires for more freedom, a chance to test abilities, to cope with the unknown. This is how children build the confidence within themselves to tackle other challenges.

When it comes to school, listen carefully to what your child has to say, discriminating between the superficial and significant. Just being a sympathetic listener will take care of transient concerns like an upcoming field trip, a test or recitation, or even a first date. Your child needs to air these concerns, but they are not a signal for you to rush to school or to intervene.

However, when you hear repeated allusions to threats and thievery and some of the other terrors of school, you should talk these over with your child's teacher or principal. Or when a child frequently forgets to turn in homework, to bring books to class, or to take assignments home, you should recognize these as manifestations of classroom-generated stress. You need to identify the areas of work where your child is feeling inadequate and decide with the help of the teacher what are the appropriate steps to take. Help at home? Tutoring? Testing?

Finally, love your child unconditionally. Conditional love—when your child feels that his parents' love for him is connected to achievement in school, to prowess with a musical instrument or on the sports field—is perhaps the greatest cause of stress in children. Conditional love is earned love, and children are afraid of losing this. Unconditional love allows your child to cope and to handle the setbacks that occur in everyone's life. When he can do that, he will be a productive and stress-free child—and your rewards will be many.

V. THE RELATIONSHIP OF HANDWRITING TO SELF-ESTEEM

In the not very distant past, there were times when it would seem that the be-all and end-all of a third or fourth grader's classroom experience was handwriting. In fact, there were students who got the impression that the state of their handwriting determined their status as a student. Well, times do change, and handwriting may have gone the way of the typewriter, although I'd like to think that it's possible that handwriting is considered important in some students' homes and classrooms.

Year after year, I met children with the self-perception that they were failing, when actually they were often students who were working on or above-grade level. How often a student, more than likely a boy, labors over a written assignment until it suits him, turns it in with an air of happy confidence, only to hear the teacher comment, "My, John. This paper isn't very neat. Couldn't you have done better?" or "John, this paper is a mess! How am I ever going to read it?" Nowhere is John hearing, "My, John. What an interesting story you wrote! I like the way you decided to end it. I put a few question marks where I couldn't understand what you had written. Could you write your next paper on a computer?"

Students' written work always needs constructive comments. References to handwriting are seldom among them. Neatness and legibility are certainly admirable accomplishments, but when we take a long look at the whole picture of a child's education, we can surely see that compared to all the skills and concepts that a child needs to master in order to be a productive adult, handwriting is far down on the scale of importance.

It becomes even less important when we recognize the damage that is inflicted by a teacher's or a parent's constant focus on handwriting instead of the content of the written work. In fact, the child may well develop a whole mental block or an attitude of indifference about writing anything! It is my firm belief that when a youngster demonstrates difficulty with handwriting, some measure of remediation should be tried. However, if the handwriting does not improve, it is best to ignore it.

Parents and teachers should explore alternative ways of getting ideas down on paper. Students can learn to do their written work both at home and in the classroom on computers. Out in the work world where we all eventually have to function, we take advantage of all the gadgets that today's technology offers. Most of us who write frequently wouldn't dream of writing by hand—even if our handwriting is perfectly beautiful. Why isn't it just as sensible to allow youngsters access to these tools?

CHAPTER II

▼

ESSENTIAL ENGLISH ELEMENTS
Rules of grammar, punctuation, parts of speech, spelling

"Even today — subjected as we are to the apotheosis of popular culture — using English respectfully helps us maintain a sense of ourselves and our values. To do otherwise, to disregard the ways of our words, is to forsake our humanity and, perhaps, even forfeit our future. A society is generally as lax as its speech. And in a society of this sort, easiness and mediocrity are much esteemed." **The Vocabula Review**

I. AN EXPLANATION OF OUR ENGLISH LANGUAGE COMPONENTS

A. Unlike Latin, English is not a dead language. It is a dynamic one derived from many sources. The following should explain some of the whys and wherefores of the disparate sounds and spellings that mold our language's lexicon.

   Once we understand prefixes, roots, and suffixes, the reasons for words such as "disappoint" being spelled with only one "s" and two "p's" and "misspell" having two "s's" will become apparent.

B. How The English Language Developed In The Past And Still Grows

   1. From original sounds:
      a. Bow-wow or echo theory; onomatopoeia: murmur, buzz
      b. Pooh-pooh theory: ugh! wow!
      c. By agreeing that certain sounds were to symbolize certain things

   2. From development within the Indo-European family of language from German through Old English (OE) and Middle English (ME) to modern English

3. From mixes of Norse and Roman mythological gods' names
   a.   Monday: Moon's day
   b.   Tuesday: Tiw (Norse God of War)'s day
   c.   Wednesday: Woden (Norse father of the gods)'s day
   d.   Thursday: Thor's day
   e.   Friday: Frigga (Woden's wife)'s day
   f.   Saturday: Saturn's day
   g.   January: Janus
   h.   March: Mars
   i.   April: From Latin *aperire*, to open
   j.   September—December: 7th, 8th, 9th, and 10th months, respectively, under the old Roman calendar

4.   From, trades, professions, places of residence, physical descriptions, sons of... we created family/surnames:
   a.   Trades: Baxter, Brewster, Chandler, Cooper, Cutler, Dyer, Farrier, Franklin, Mason, Miller, Sawyer, Shepherd, Smith, Wainwright
   b.   Professions: Clark (Clerk), Duke, Mayer (Meyer), Parson, Priest
   c.   Place of residence: Bridges, Brooks, Hill
   d.   Physical descriptions: Brown, Russell, Stout, Long
   e.   Sons of: Anderson; Jonson; Adkins (son of Adam); Peterkin; Dixon, Ivanovitch (Russian, son of Ivan); MacDonald, McPhey (Scotch and Irish); O' (Irish) O'Brien; Van, Von (Dutch, German): Van Buren; De (French): DeHaven; Ben (Hebrew), Ben Gurion

5. From natural and man-made locations
   a.   -burg, -burgh, -bury (borough/fort): Parkersburg, Pittsburgh, Newbury
   b.   -chester, -cester, -caster (Roman for fort or camp): Portchester, Worcester, Lancaster
   c.   -dale (valley): Scottsdale, Scarsdale, Hartsdale
   d.   field: Springfield
   e.   ford: Hartford, Waterford, Chelmsford, Haverford
   f.   –ham: Teutonic origin; a cluster of houses in the country, especially belonging to a parish or village: Birmingham, Nottingham, Chatham, Eastham
   g.   -haven: New Haven, Bremerhaven
   h.   -land: Scotland, Maryland
   i.   -mont (mountain): Egremont, Beaumont, Piedmont

j. -port (harbor, safe place): Newport
k. -ton, -town (town): Newton, Washington, Georgetown
l. -ville (French for town): Andersonville, Jacksonville, Nashville
m. -wich, -wick (Latin, *vicus*, for village): Sandwich, Southwick
n. cities named for people: Washington, Louisville, Jefferson, Lincoln
o. American Indian place names: Adirondack, Agawam, Canada, Chicago, Illinois
p. Made-up names: Texarkana (Texas + Arkansas + Louisiana); Kenova, West Virginia (Kentucky + Ohio +Virginia); Delmarva Peninsula (Delaware + Maryland + Virginia)

6. By borrowing from other languages:
    a. Spanish: fiesta, patio
    b. French: parachute, chauffeur, crochet
    c. Latin: *et cetera, post scriptum*, appendix
    d. Greek: psalm, chaos, lynx
    e. American Indian: chipmunk, moccasin, hickory
    f. German: kindergarten, quartz, sauerkraut
    g. Arabic: adobe, harem, sheik
    h. Other: khaki, hari-kari, berserk

7. By applying etymological significance to trade names (Magnavox®), new products (Cascade®), scientific terms (megaton, quadraphonic), and newly-coined words (sit-in, brainwash)

8. By combining two common words: Handbag, housetop, newspaper

9. By shortening formerly-used terms: Gym (gymnasium), bus (omnibus), 'coon (raccoon)

10. By blending: Twirl (twist & swirl), splatter (splash & spatter), smog (smoke & fog)

11. By creating acronyms: ZIP (Zoning Improvement Plan), SRO (Standing Room Only), GOP (Grand Old Party)—and possibly 100's more!

12. By naming or describing:
    a. Scientific discoveries: Electronics, megaton, quasar

Probe and Shed Light

        b.   Particular places: Newcastle (by the new castle), Springfield (spring by the field)

        c   New situations: Black Power, sit-in, cold war

        d.   Household products: Bon Ami®: French for good friend; <u>Aqua</u> Velva®: Soft water; <u>Minitran</u>®: Small + transportation unit, like a van or bus. Find more of these on page 90.

13. By just being original: Kodak*, peanuttiest*, uncola*

14. By using the names of famous men: America (from the Latinized version of the explorer **Amerigo** Vespucci's name); George **Pullman**, who invented the Pullman sleeping car; Robert **Bunsen**, a chemist who created the Bunsen Burner. Can you add to these names?

15. By using descriptive place names: **Calico**, material originally made in Calicut, India; **Jersey**, the largest of the Channel Islands, where a soft cloth made from wool, cotton, or silk originated; **Paisley**, a cotton material made in Scotland using the droplet-shaped vegetable motif, or a twisted teardrop, of Persian and Indian origin

16. By taking the names of characters from literature:
        a.   Bible: He's a Nimrod/Job/Jonah.
        b.   Fiction: That's a Cinderella story. He's a Scrooge. She met her Prince Charming. She's the Ugly Duckling of the family.
        c.   Mythology (Greek, Roman, Norse): George surely found his Achilles heel.

17. By limiting language to a group: A fin: Five dollars. Make goo-goo eyes: To look amorously at someone. He tanked: He failed.

18. By bringing new meanings to old words, such as cool, square, tough.

Bookmark these exceptionally helpful sites:
http://www.wordsources.info/words-for-modern-age.html
http://www.bartleby.com/59/

II.   THE PRESCRIPTS FOR ENGLISH WRITING

Learning to write declarative, interrogative, imperative, and exclamatory sentences, as well as simple, compound, complex, and compound-complex sentences are important concepts for students as they progress to higher grades. At the appropriate time, train students to use proper punctuation, capitalization, nouns and pronouns in agreement, subjects and verbs in agreement, and introductory (non-dangling) clauses. Provide opportunities for narrative, expository, descriptive, and persuasive writing. Require research that uses dictionaries, encyclopedias, atlases, almanacs, and the Internet. The outline of these elements below will help you organize lesson plans.

Although the teaching of grammar appears to have been lost somewhere in the education process, I feel it is an important element of every child's learning. In many cases, teachers and parents themselves do not know the rules of grammar and punctuation, and, therefore, cannot teach it to their students. I hope the synopsis of grammar I present below will fill this need.

Much of this chapter's substance is to provide teachers and parents with innovative material to assist students in learning, to solve students' grammar and punctuation problems, and to introduce new elements into existing educational materials. I hope you will find ways to utilize my strategies and techniques, as proficiency in them separates those who are educated from those who aren't, an important asset in the world of work. Submitting an errorless résumé and speaking correctly during an interview are likely to make a positive impression on prospective employers.

A. Mechanics
   1. **Sentences: Four basic types** with examples and proper end punctuation:
      a. **Declarative**: States a fact or opinion. This year school ended on May 30.
      b. **Interrogative**: Asks/raises a question. Did school end on May 30?
      c. **Exclamatory**: Expresses a strong feeling. Thankfully, school ended on May 30!
      d. **Imperative**: End school on May 30!

   2. **All must have a subject (a naming part) and a predicate (a telling part).**
      School (subject) closed (telling). In an imperative sentence, the subject is not said or written but is understood to be you. (You) Close school!

a. Subjects and predicates may have more than one word. <u>The small</u> <u>elementary school</u> (complete subject) <u>closed on May 30</u> (complete predicate). <u>Subjects</u> and <u>predicates</u> may be compound. <u>Mel and</u> <u>Dana</u> <u>ran and jumped all the way home</u>.

b. Simple subjects are only one word, either a noun* or pronoun*; simple predicates consist of a verb*. <u>School</u> <u>closed</u> on May 30.

3. **Compound sentences** are two complete sentences joined by a conjunction or connecting word (and, but, or, nor) and separated by a comma. **There** **is a subject both before and after the conjunction**. <u>School</u> <u>closed</u> on May 30 this year, and <u>it</u> <u>will reopen</u> on September 6. The following sentence is not a compound sentence because there is no subject after the "and". <u>School</u> <u>closed</u> in May and <u>will reopen</u> in September; there is a compound verb (closed and will reopen).

4. **Egregious errors:**

a. **Run-on sentences** occur when proper punctuation is not used. School closed in May, students were happy. A comma by itself cannot hold those two statements together. (See semicolon.)

b. **Sentence fragments** (broken pieces) happen when a sentence (1) does not have both a subject and a predicate (A tall man with a red beard), or (2) does not make sense by itself (Because he dyed his beard red). See: http://grammar.ccc.commnet.edu/grammar/ http://www.emints.org/ethemes/resources/S00001595.shtml

c. **Split infinitives:** An infinitive will almost always begin with "to," and will be followed by a verb, as in: to walk, to think, to spend. However, when another word comes between these "partners," it splits the infinitive. Here are two examples:
    1. to slowly walk
    2. to finally think (of an answer)
    3. to badly behave

How can you fix these?
    a. He made it clear to not cross the white line.
    b. The balloon began to slowly drop.
    c. He went to frantically call his daughter.

(See Appendix for answers.)

4. **Incorrect connections between singular and plural subjects and verbs.** Watch for nouns, such as *none* (think *not one*) and *neither, each, everyone, everybody*, all of which are **singular** and often have an intervening prepositional phrase between their subjects and verbs: none ... is; each of the girls ... is; everyone ... is; 30media are plural—the data in my report are correct; the media were there.
   http://www.chompchomp.com/terms/infinitive.htm
   http://www.testmagic.com/grammar/explanations/verbs/split-infinitives.asp
   http://www.bartleby.com/64/C001/059.html

5. **Misstating facts:** The writers of these newspaper statements appear to be protecting the drivers, rather than stating, "Two injured when driver drove his truck into a building."
   a. Two injured when truck crashed into building.
   b. His car crossed Route 22 and hit a tree. (Where was the driver?)

B. **Clauses**: If a clause can stand alone as a sentence, it is an independent clause. However, if it cannot stand alone, it is a dependent or subordinate clause, subordinated to another part of the sentence and often beginning with words such as if, whether, since, etc.
   See: http://grammar.ccc.commnet.edu/grammar/clauses.htm.

1. **Independent clauses** must have a subject and a verb. We closed school because it was very hot. Put the clause first, however, and a comma must follow. Because it was very hot, we closed school.

2. **Dependent / subordinate clause**: Because it was very hot, we closed school. Various signals can start these: How? On what condition? Why?

3. **For noun, adjective, and adverbial clauses, see:**
   http://faculty.deanza.edu/flemingjohn/stories/storyReader$23;
   www.uottawa.ca/academic/arts/writcent/hypergrammar/bldcls.html

   a. Show:
      1. Possessives of nouns: Mary's hat, more than one birds' bath, the day's weather, James's coat, two days' drive, Jane and Ann's room

 2. The omission of letters: don't (do not), didn't (did not), could've (could **have**, NOT could **of**)

 b. Do <u>not</u> use an apostrophe in the years of a decade or a century: The 1990s, the 1400s

C. Punctuation
 1. End punctuation (see A, 1 a-d above)
 2. Internal punctuation:
  a. **Commas**

   1. Words in a series: Sue bought cakes, pies, cookies* and drinks for the party. *optional comma

   2. Around appositives: Miss Jones, *my English teacher*, was tall.

   3. In compound sentences: See A3.

   4. After introductory prepositional phrases: For the party, Sue bought cakes and pies. Before buying, Sue took a vote on people's choices. (on) The day Sue went, she had to hurry.

   5. After introductory phrases: Having been elected, Sue went right to work.

   6. After introductory or dependent clauses above.

   7. Around interrupting phrases: Sue, along with two friends, made posters. Sue, we knew, would do a great job.

   8. In dialogue: (1) Sue asked, "When does school start?" (2) No punctuation needed: Sue asked me when school started. (3) "I hope school does not start while it's still hot," she remarked. "I hope," remarked Sue, "that school does not start soon." **Note**: End punctuation goes inside the quotation mark, not after.

   9. In dates and addresses: Clinton, Iowa, is a small city. Sue started work on, September 10, 2007, in the cafeteria.

10. Stress "however." We were, however, not surprised that Sue worked so hard. Sue worked hard; however, we weren't surprised. (Without the semicolon, this would be a run-on sentence. Sue worked hard is a complete sentence, as is: However, we weren't surprised.)

11. When <u>not</u> to use a comma: When there is no subject after a conjunction, i.e., Clinton, Iowa, is a small city <u>but has</u> many parks.

b. Semicolons(;) separate:

1. Main clauses not joined by a coordinating conjunction: Sue went to work; she took the bus.

2. Phrases or clauses containing commas, even when joined by coordinating conjunctions. Sue worked on the books, desks* and chairs; Tom cleaned the floor and walls; Joan did whatever else was needed. *A comma here is optional.

c. **Colons** (:) mark a pause for explanation, expansion, enumeration, or elaboration. Use a colon to introduce a list. Sue did a lot of work: She shopped, took a vote, made posters.

d. Apostrophes

1. With contractions: <u>He's</u> a great friend. <u>Don't</u> go near the stove. That <u>isn't</u> safe.

2. To show possession: <u>Tom's</u> hat; a <u>child's</u> toy; the Chavez's car; the <u>puss's</u> tail

3. <u>James's</u>* ball; <u>Diaz's</u> father
   * Last *s* is not necessary; it's a matter of choice.

4. The four <u>homeschoolers'</u> papers; ten girls' stories; those women's coats; the Sanchez's house

5. The House-in-the-Meadow's Inn has 30 rooms.

6. Use the apostrophe and *s* after the second name when two people possess the same item: *Cesar and Maribel's home* is constructed of redwood. However, for separate ownership:
    Cesar's and Maribel's contracts will be renewed next year.

7. Never use an apostrophe with possessive pronouns: *his, hers, its, theirs, ours, yours, whose.* They already show possession so they do not require an apostrophe. That book is hers, not yours.

8. The plurals for capital letters and numbers used as nouns are not formed with apostrophes.
    a. She consulted with *three M.D.s.*
    b. **BUT** She went to *three M.D.s' offices.* The apostrophe is needed here to show plural possession.
    c. She learned her ABCs; the 1990s **not** the 1990's
    d. She learned her times tables for 6s and 7s.

D. Parts of Speech

1. **Common noun**: A person (sister), place (park), or thing (ball)

2. **Proper noun**: The specific name of a person (Mary), place (New York), or **thing** (World Trade Center)

3. **Pronoun**: A word (he, she, it) used in place of a noun (boy, Mary, kite)

4. **Verb**: The critical element of the predicate says something about the subject of the sentence and expresses action, and the present, past, or future time. Mary **talks** a lot. Mary **talked** to me yesterday. She **will talk** at the meeting.

5. A **present participle** is a verb ending in *-ing*, and is called dangling when the subject of the *-ing* verb and the subject of the sentence do not agree. For example: "Rushing to finish her work, the broom slipped out of Sue's hand." Here the subject is the broom, but the broom isn't doing the rushing.

6. **Adjective**: A word that modifies a noun or a pronoun; it answers which one, how many, or what kind. The **slippery** broom flew out of Sue's hands.

7. **Adverb**: Modifies a verb and answers in what manner, to what degree: When, how, how many times. The broom flew **suddenly** from Sue's hands.

E. **Gerunds, Participles, and Infinitives:**
   http://owl.english.purdue.edu/owl/resource/627/01/
   www.chompchomp.com/terms/participle.htm

F. **References**:
   1. **Grammar and style**:
      http://www.andromeda.rutgers.edu/~jlynch/Writing/
      http://www.comfit.com/grammar/: "A fitness-center approach"
      http://www.grammarnow.com/
      http://www.grammarbook.com/
      http://www.protrainco.com/info/grammar.htm
      http://www.wsu.edu/~brians/errors/errors.html
      http://www.dailygrammar.com/
      http://www.edufind.com/english/grammar/

   2. **Punctuation:**
      http://www.arts.uottawa.ca/writcent/hypergrammar/punct.html
      http://grammar.ccc.commnet.edu/grammar/marks/marks.htm
      http://owl.english.purdue.edu/handouts/grammar/

   3. **Parts of speech**, especially well-reinforced by diagramming sentences:
      http://www.sta.cathedral.org/lowerschool/form1/eng1javwww/Grammar/Diagramming/
      http://www.lifestreamcenter.net/DrB/Lessons/TS/diagram.htm
      http://www.redshift.com/~bonajo/diagram.htm (excellent!)
      www.uottawa.ca/academic/arts/writcent/hypergrammar/arts/ writcent/hypergrammar/

III.   GRAMMAR'S TENACIOUS TRAPS

"Good grammar, in the fullest sense of the term, is neither an embellishment nor an accessory to anything else. It is the Law by which meaning is found and made. It may be, of course, that a good "education" ought to provide something more, but it is preposterous, perhaps even wicked, to suggest that it can be had with anything less."

Richard Mitchell

A. **Bad vs badly**: You feel *bad* when you are expressing a sentiment or emotion. To say, "I feel badly," implies that there's something wrong with your sense of touch. This is a good matter for the WatchBird! See below on page 30.)

B. **"That" for "who"**: Be sure to use who (a subjective pronoun) when referring to a person. The principal is the one ~~that~~ **who** made the decision. He is the new teacher ~~that~~ **who** will coach football. She's the woman who… I saw the man who … Most likely, this shift has become prevalent because so many people fear using the wrong pronoun: who/whom.

C. **Who vs. Whom**: Both of these are pronouns. Who is a subject; whom is an object. To whom are you writing? Grammar Girl© has a tip to help you if you're not sure which to use: "Like *whom*, the pronoun *him* ends with *m*. When you're trying to decide whether to use *who* or *whom*, ask yourself if the answer to the question would be *he* or *him*."

D. **Unique**! Unique means "one of a kind" and cannot be modified. Absolutely <u>nothing</u> can be "~~very~~ unique" or "~~the most~~ unique" or "~~completely~~ unique"!

E. **Preventative**: She took **preventative** steps to make sure they'd be safe from the storm. Preventative **is not a word**. Preventive is!

F. **Examples**: Write these on a black/white board; review them frequently.

1. The trustees of the organization felt badly about it's poor operations, but were glad to hear that all the data was correct. **Errors**: (1) **Felt badly** means did a bad job of feeling with their fingers/hands; should be *felt bad* (2) *It's* is a contraction of it is, but in this case its, the possessive pronoun, should be used (3) No comma should appear before *but* because it is not a compound sentence; it is one sentence with a compound verb (subject:

trustees; verbs: were embarrassed and were glad) (4) Data is a plural word (datum is the singular) and should, therefore, have the plural verb, were.

2. We ordered clearly from the menu, however, the ice tea never came. **Errors**: (1) Incorrect punctuation: *however* is a conjunctive adverb in this case, not parenthetic, and as such should have either a semicolon or a period before it. As it stands, these are two run-on sentences. (2) Ice tea should be ice**d** tea.

3. He gave alot of tickets to Mary and I to use any time we wanted. **Errors**: (1) Alot is always two words: a lot; (2) "...gave tickets to Mary and I ..." should read "gave tickets to Mary and **me**." You would say, "He gave the tickets to me;" it doesn't matter that another's name comes before the pronoun *me*. Me is the object of the preposition *to*. I is a subject, not an object.

4. The garden club already held their annual meeting, and elected new officers. **Errors**: (1) Garden club is singular; therefore *their* should be *its*; (2) ... and elected ... is only a phrase, not a sentence, so there is no need for a comma.

5. **Each** of these victims thought that **they** were providing roadside assistance. (Should be **all** instead of each, or he/she instead of they.)

6. You can understand if **somebody** wants to let **themselves** deteriorate, but when **they** do this to their children and make their children suffer, that's unexplainable. "Somebody" fouled this one up! Perhaps "people" or "parents" and a plural verb would work instead. See also, #11 below: Same problem but, oh! so common! Collect these yourself and use in your classroom.

7. One day your child turns sixteen and you let them borrow the keys to the car. Your **child** is singular; **them** is plural, so they are not in agreement. Change **them** to **him or her**.

8. When I got to the party, I found her waiting **on** me. Waitresses and waiters wait **on** people. Friends wait **for** someone.

9. **It's alright for each department to set up their own program**. (1) "alright" is <u>always</u> two words: all right. (2) "...each ... set up their ..." Each is a singular subject; their is plural but is referring back to each. Sentence should read, "...each department to set up **its** own program" or "...all departments to set up their own program."

10. **He gave the news to Jim and myself.** Not completely wrong to use myself, but better to say, "He gave the news to Jim and me." I often think that whoever is speaking is not sure of the correct pronoun so goes with myself. Tell your students that they can trust "me."

11. **If a person wants to do their banking after hours, they can**. [(1) "a person" is singular; "their" is plural. Therefore, this sentence could read either, "If people want to do their banking ..." or, "If a person wants to do his/her banking..."] (2) "they," which is plural, refers back to a/one person.

12. **No parent in their right mind** would let their child hitchhike across the country. Parent is singular. Better to state it, "**Parents** in their right minds..."

13. **Everyone stops what they're doing when the siren blares.** Every<u>one</u> is singular so "they" should be "he" or "he or she." "**Everybody** managed to have **their** own bike." Everybody is singular, too; therefore, "*their own bike*" should be his/her own bike.

14. **When a customer leaves here, they feel fine.** ("a customer ... they." Yep, once again, a singular subject and a plural pronoun! How about, "When **customers** leave ...")

15. **If the worker didn't show up, we went out and got them**. ["...the worker (singular) ..." them," plural.]

16. **He and I were late to the Murphy's party**. (Turn Murphy's party into the party of the Murphys and you see that the apostrophe should come after Murphys, not between the *y* and the *s*.)

17. **The team of veterinarians have decided on a treatment**. ["team" (the sentence's subject) is singular; "have" is a plural verb, so it should read "team

…has." ("Of veterinarians" is a prepositional phrase; "veterinarians" is the object of the preposition "of" and not the subject of the sentence.)]

18. **Hopefully, they will show up, so we don't have to look for them**. I know this will be a shock to many people since *hopefully* is well entrenched in many people's vocabulary, but it is not correct when used this way. "Hopefully" is an adverb and must modify a verb, which in this sentence, it does not. It is better to say, "We hope they ..." or "I hope ..." Hopefully means in a hopeful manner, as in, "We are hopefully waiting for a sunny day."

19. **Nobody has received their letter yet.** ("nobody"=singular); ("their"=plural; try: Not one of us has...)

20. **Brighten someone's day today by making them breakfast**. (Nice try, but <u>someone</u> is <u>singular</u>, so them, plural, cannot refer to someone or even somebody. Substitute "him" or "her" for 'them".

21. **He told me to quickly go out the door before the police arrived**. ("To go" is an infinitive. Putting any word between the two parts of an infinitive is *splitting an infinitive*. The sentence should say, "He told me to go quickly....")

22. Here are a few I ripped from the daily newspaper. Can you pick out the error in each? How should each sentence have read?

   a.   I never saw a bit of a problem between he or his wife.

   b.   I wanted to see if anyone's interests would be peaked.

   c.   Both her and her husband forgot about it.

   d.   There's several things in there that indicate to myself and the district attorney that suggest mental health issues.

   e.   Every one of us has done something they regret.

   f.   Help needed finding critically missing man.

Answers in Appendix on Page 223

Probe and Shed Light

For some good laughs, read ***Fumblerules*** by William Safire, online: <u>http://www.wku.</u> <u>edu/tlc/For%20New%20TLC%20Site/fumblrules_of_writing.htm</u> : (humorous rules for writing, collected from teachers of English grammar, i.e. "Avoid run-on sentences they are hard to read.")

IV. SPELLING: Remedies for Persistent Errors

> *"The knowledge imposes a pattern...*
> *for the pattern is new in every moment."*
> T. S. Eliot

I am often asked why I make a "big deal" out of correct spelling. Today it is often not taught as a separate subject, and children feel it's not important because "spell check" will catch their errors. Unfortunately, it doesn't catch wrong usage or words that sound alike but have different meanings, nor has it truly taught them anything. I think the quality of a person's spelling reflects his general knowledge of English, which will matter when an employer expects correctness in all aspects of English.

I'm sure most of us have noticed how correct spelling comes easily to some students but is difficult for others. Intelligence plays no part in this, as illustrated by my college roommate, a brilliant girl in pre-med studies, a versatile piano player, and a whiz at card games—and the worst speller imaginable.

For many years I've analyzed reasons behind incorrect spellings, along with ways to help poor spellers become better ones. First of all, I see a correlation between those who excel in arithmetic and those who spell well. Both of these areas of learning are dependent upon good visual memory. Most good spellers rely upon a word "looking right."

Although spelling may a bit easier today with computer technology that flags a misspelled word, this usually does not help poor spellers. Furthermore, teachers and parents tell me that with the widespread use texting* and emailing*, today's children can barely begin to put pen to paper. Most cannot write a sentence, never mind an essay, so spelling correctly is not a top concern for them. Nonetheless, we cannot shrug off our responsibility to encourage our children to become proficient spellers.

If spelling is one of your child's difficult subjects and you are not his teacher, there are ways you can help at home. Find out from the teacher the schedule that spelling lessons follow. In most cases, one lesson per week is covered in a spelling text or workbook, starting on Monday and ending with a test on Friday. Assuming that this is the pattern in your child's class, on the weekend utilize the teaching strategy of a pretest by dictating any word from the week's upcoming lesson that you think anyone could possibly misspell

One problem that creates misspellings is when students write what think they hear. (See often misinterpreted words below.) Together, you should analyze the words to understand how or why anyone might misspell them. Take long words syllable by syllable. Might an incorrect homonym (two or more words that sound alike but have different meanings, such as there and their or hear and here) have been used? Do some words have silent letters? Was there a tricky word with two possible spellings (*sight, site*)?

In order to make sure that students understand the meaning of each week's words, they may need to write or state the words in sentences. You can also accomplish two goals with one assignment by requiring students to meld current and previous vocabulary words with the spelling sentences. If you train your students to underline the spelling words, you will be able to spot them quickly.

Afterwards, check these words together. Ask children to analyze the type of error: Was a syllable left out? A rule of phonics not followed, i.e., when a word that has a short vowel (*plan*) is put into the past tense, the end consonant must be doubled (*planned*) or the vowel will become a long sound (*planed*)? Was one vowel substituted for another? Was it a tricky word with two possible spellings (*exceed* or *excede*)? Sometimes what you hear is not what you get when you spell (*pedestal* sounds more like *pedastal*; *extrovert* sounds like *extravert* and so on). This conscious focus on the error is important as it leads to comprehension. All year, concentrate on those that are often misspelled (it's, its; there, their, they're, etc.).

As a parent, keep a list of all words missed by your children on tests, so that you can review them often. One way to make this fun is to compose sentences that use as many of the missed words as possible. They may be a bit silly, but they get the job done! While you're at it, throw in as many of the confusing homonyms as you can: "its and it's," "where and wear," "there, their, they're," etc.

The frequently misspelled and misspoken words below occur because the writers or speakers are not aware of the endings as indicated by numbers 1, 2, 3, such as the almost silent "d" at the end of a word, which is "swallowed" by the speaker and thus is barely heard. Others shown below are similar to the first three but are the result of the writer/listener not being aware of the make-up of contractions. These errors are especially common among those for whom English is a second language, as well as those who've heard them all their lives, which some today consider to be a recognized dialect, an accepted vernacular. Listen carefully for these mistakes when your students are talking.

Today, we face the problem of keeping "like" out of everyday language! Like, you know what I mean. Right?

* http://www.160characters.org/documents/SocialEffectsOfTextMessaging.pdf;
* http://www.timesonline.co.uk/tol/life_and_style/education/student/news/article384086.ece;
* http://www.associatedcontent.com/article/783729/the_negative_effects_of_text_messaging.html?cat=7

A.   **Often misinterpreted words.** When dictating these sentences don't emphasize the "d" or "t" or the second "u" on the underlined words.

    1.   The truck carried an <u>oversized</u> load.
    2.   She served <u>iced</u> tea.
    3.   It was an <u>old-fashioned</u> idea.
    4.   I was <u>supposed</u> to be home by four.
    5.   He <u>kept</u> the ball for himself.
    6.   I <u>usually</u> get up at seven
    7.   He <u>asked</u> if he could watch the TV.
    8.   I <u>halved</u> the apple for the children.

B.   The following show contentious—almost silent—contractions for has, have, would, will, been, is. State them as they are often spoken. Swallow those in bold type.

    1.   We should'**ve** gone with them. (Expect to see "should of.")
    2.   I would **of** (have) gone if it hadn't rained.
    3.   Who'd **of** (have) thought she was only sixteen?
    4.   I (**'ve**) seen him.
    5.   He (**'s**) done it many times.
    6.   It ('ll) be hot today.
    7.   I ('ll)) be there when I sposed (supposed) to be.
    8.   We ('re) coming to pick you up.
    9.   He ('d) be here if his brother hadn't died.
    10. He ('s) one big man!
    11. Who ('s) gonna (going to) be there?
    12. She have no idea where I am. (Have and has sound so much alike that they may be confused.)

C.   **Then, there's just plain nonstandard English**
    1.   Then, like, the cable broke.

2. This be too heavy for me. (be instead of is)
3. I seen it. (seen instead of saw)
4. She didn't have no legs cause, like, the accident cut them off.

Students who are consistently accurate spellers could forego further formal instruction. Instead, they should keep a personal spelling book containing errors from any of their writing. Once in a while you can test these students on their own misspelled words. Those not taking the weekly test should have a book or other work at hand to occupy them while others are working on the test.

Many words confuse students who are not well grounded on long and short vowel sounds. For instance:

cuter	cutter
dining	dinning (as in a noise)
griping	gripping
hoping	hopping
mated	matted
planed	planned
shiny	shinny

D. Remedies For Misspelled Words

1. Have children write misspelled words in context, that is, in a short sentence. By using these as they will in future writing, they will gain mastery.

2. Keep a list of all misspelled words, so that you can review them often. One way to make this fun is to compose sentences that use as many of these persistent errors as possible. They may be a bit silly, but they get the job done! While you're at it, throw in a bunch of confusing homonyms: "its and it's," "where and wear," "there, their, they're," etc.

3. Use a "Watchbird"

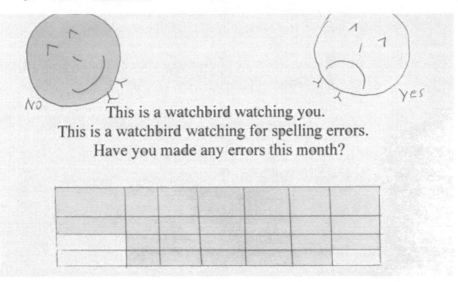

This is a watchbird watching you.
This is a watchbird watching for spelling errors.
Have you made any errors this month?

When students make repetitious errors in spelling, punctuation, and other elements of writing, make a "Watchbird" chart similar to that of a child's weekly task sheet. Knowing that it is "watching" them will cause them to pay more attention to their errors. Most students become motivated to get all NOs from the Watchbird.

Create a Watchbird at the top of an 8 ½ "X 11" as shown above and put it in the front of the classroom. This may sound overly simple, but it worked for all my students, especially those is middle school. They paid more attention to their work because they did not want their names to be under the "Yes" Watchbird.

This is a WATCHBIRD watching YOU!
This is a WATCHBIRD watching for YOUR ERRORS!
Have you made any errors this WEEK/MONTH?

Draw lines down the rest of the page where you can put dates and type of errors or a solid NO!.

4. Prevent Pitiful Pitfalls

While focusing on words that students commonly misspell (my "pitiful pitfalls"), challenge students who are ready for work that goes beyond their standard grade expectations by selecting higher level "pitiful pitfalls." Add to these words as needs arise.

Probe and Shed Light

Another effective method to improve students' performance on grade-level words is to make a chart of these words, checking them off when the class reaches 100%. Dictate sentences each of which contains several of these worrisome words, eg: "*On* <u>Tuesday</u>, *the four* <u>friends</u> <u>chose</u> *many* <u>pretty</u> *colors for their* <u>clothes</u>." "*The* <u>principal's</u> <u>knowledge</u> *of* <u>restaurants</u> *and* <u>picnicking</u> *spots was* <u>unbelievable</u>!

Pitiful Pitfalls by Grades;

Grades 1-2
been
choose
coming
does
four
friend
goes
many
once
one
pretty
three
two
when

Grades 3-4—all above, plus:
all right (<u>never</u> alright!)
calendar
clothes
color
coming
doesn't
handkerchief
library
loose
lose
ocean
people
piece
receive
remember

school
tomorrow
used
women

Grades 5-6—all above, plus:
because
believe
carrot
cooperate
decision
doubt
etc.
fierce
grateful
knowledge
misspell
picnicking
probably
rabbit
realize
rhyme
rhythm
science
secretary
sheriff
skiing
special
squirrel
studying
though
thought

through
trophy
usually
valuable
weird
young

Grades 7 - 8—all above, plus:
Arctic
artificial
cemetery
embarrassment
Europe
restaurant
specimen
weird

For all grades:

a. **Weekdays**
Tuesday
Wednesday
Thursday
Saturday

b. **Months**
January
February
August

c. **North American Cities**
Chicago
Los Angeles
Milwaukee
Philadelphia
Pittsburgh
San Francisco
Tallahassee
Tucson, etc.

d. **North American States**
Arkansas
Connecticut
Delaware
Hawaii
Illinois
Louisiana
Maryland
Massachusetts
Michigan
Minnesota
Pennsylvania
Rhode Island
South Dakota
Tennessee
Utah
Wisconsin

e. **Great Lakes**: From smallest to largest: Recite, spell, or write
Ontario
Eire
Michigan
Huron
Superior

f. **Continents**: Recite and spell, or write
Africa
Antarctica
Asia
Australia
Europe
North America
South America

V. PREPARING FOR A WRITING ASSIGNMENT*

"Minds are like parachutes. They only function when they are open."
James Dewar

A. **The Process of Good Writing:** Have students practice multiple sentences and paragraphs using elements 1-7 below.

1. **Decide the type of writing you will use:**
   a. Expository: Write to inform by giving facts, explaining something, defining something, giving directions.
   b. Narrative: Tell your reader what happened, how and when – real or imagined. Use dialogue in imaginative ways, such as one car "talking" to another. Study a portrait, such as the "Mona Lisa," "The Laughing Cavalier", someone on the cover of a magazine, or others your find elsewhere: What were those people thinking? What would they tell you if they could talk?
   c. Descriptive: Tell how something looked, felt, sounded, smelled or tasted—real or imagined.
   d. Persuasive: Convince the reader to think about something or to do something. Use logic and/or emotional appeals.

2. **Determine who your audience (your reader) is**: A friend, your entire class, a parent, a businessperson, etc.

3. **Make a word cluster around your topic**: That is, put your topic inside a circle in the center of a paper, then write any ideas that come to mind around the topic, joining each by a line that connects it to the central topic. Some of your ideas may be related to other ideas; attach these sub-ideas to the main one. Now you have a focus for your writing project.

4. **Use an active voice (verb) instead of a passive one**. With the active voice, the subject <u>performs</u> the action expressed in the verb; in the passive voice, the subject <u>receives</u> the action, which usually weakens the impact of your writing. Instead of, "I was called by the doctor." (passive), write, "The doctor called me." (active). Active verbs represent "doing;" passive verbs show something being done to another. Other passive statements: No odor was detected. The pin was bought at Macy's, instead of, "He bought the pin at Macy's. Forms of "to be" (is, are, am, was, were, has

been, have been, had been, will be, will have been) **plus** a past participle (adding -d or -ed to the root form of the verb) creates a passive voice.

Can you rephrase these from passive statements to active ones? **(a)** "A difference can be made by you." **(b)** "The ball was caught by Marie." **(c)** "Michael was missed by his mother." (d) "She can be contacted at 443-962-5055."

Active answers: (a) "You can make a difference." **(b)** "Marie caught the ball." **(c)** "Michael's mother missed him." (d) "Contact her at 443-962-5055." Check your writing frequently to make sure you are expressing yourself in the best manner.

5. **Check your grammar:** Review **page 16** for reminders on how to avoid egregious errors, such as, "None were seen speeding." "A GPS could help better track his movements."

6. **Write the first draft of your work**, incorporating all your ideas in your cluster.

7. **Read your work over critically. Be sure your writing says exactly what you want it to. Change your words, order of ideas, or whatever it takes to make your meaning clear. Rewrite as often as necessary.**

8. **Check** all spelling, capitalization, and punctuation.

9. **Avoid clichés and hackneyed phrases; they're "old hat!"** Overused words and phrases are tiring after a while. Be more original than:
    a. "We're on the same page."
    b. "At that point in time...": Just say then or now.
    c. "24-7."
    d. "It's a worst case scenario."
    e. "It was a judgment call."
    f. "She was thinking outside the box."
    g. "His injury is not considered life threatening." Why not just say "serious"?
    h. "On day one...,"
    i. He is "A person of interest." Suspect is better.

B. 101 Ways (PLUS 3) To Choose a Writing Topic

*"One crucial goal of education is to rouse and
stimulate the love of mental adventure."*
Bertrand Russell

1. Sentence Starters to Develop Into Paragraphs or Themes (1-20)

- I feel proud when ...
- I look forward to ...
- On weekends I most like to ...
- I feel bad when ...
- I often worry about ...
- I wish people wouldn't ...
- I was never so embarrassed in my life as when ...
- My hair stood on end when ...
- I would have had a good time at the party except ...
- When I am a parent, I will never ...
- If I ruled the world, I ...
- My favorite season of the year is_____ . (Explain why you chose that season and what you might see, hear, smell, touch.)
- In ten years, I will probably be ...
- The type of person I most dislike is one who...
- The type of person I most admire is one who ...
- If my great-great grandfather could come back for a visit today, he would be amazed by ...
- The greatest airplane ever built is ...
- My favorite way to spend a weekend is ...
- I was proud of myself when I ...
- Dad was surely angry after ...

2. Topics to Develop Into Stories: (21-43)

- My funniest dream
- My most delightful dream
- My worst nightmare
- When I was a hero (fictional or real one)
- As a baby-sitter, I've had many experiences
- Washing my dog

- Moving to a new house
- What I do when I am lonely
- The happiest day I can remember
- The first time I ever babysat/rode a bike/went swimming/baked a cake/ spent a night away from home ...
- My life as an apple core
- My hide-away
- My biggest worry
- How I earn money
- Sounds I like
- How bees make honey
- Life in an ant colony
- My best friend
- My favorite teacher (now or in the past)
- The things I like are blue / red / yellow / _____.
- I can usually find lots to do on rainy days.
- Sometimes a little brother can be a nuisance.
- Sometimes a little sister can be a nuisance.

3. **Topic Sentences to Develop into Paragraphs or Themes: (44-74)**

- Boys' hairstyles are getting weirder every year.
- Children need lots of discipline while growing up.
- It is good for everyone to follow some religion.
- I can be helpful around the house in many ways.
- Everyone should have a hobby.
- It is better to have friends than lots of money.
- I would rather wear a uniform to school than my own clothes.
- I would rather wear my own clothes to school than a uniform.
- Every child should have a regular allowance.
- Boys have more fun than girls.
- Girls have more fun than boys.
- Giving can bring as much pleasure as receiving.
- The holiday my family enjoyed the best was ...
- The reasons I or others bully.*
- Shoes tell a great deal about a person. *
- I think the greatest danger to mankind is _____ because _____

_____

- There are many reasons why another cat will not take up residence in my home.
- It is dangerous to be living in this country today.
- Although bike riding / swimming / baby-sitting / another activity is one of my favorite activities, it is not without its problems.
- I have always wanted (name a pet) because_____.
- Sometimes a party, which is meant to be fun, is really dreadful.
- Children should / should not have homework every night.
- One day when I was a little boy / girl, I had a frightening experience.
- Beer advertising on television should be abolished.
- To wash your dog properly, you must follow several steps.
- Being short / tall isn't always an advantage.
- Success comes after hard work.
- A wagon, a rainy day, two children, a good-natured pup ... **
- Bees, hens, a blossoming apple tree, a copy of Harry Potter, a girl, a field mouse ...
- A clock on the corner, a school bus, heavy school books, bulky overshoes, slippery footing ... **
- A sailboat on a lake, a large storm cloud, two children and a dog... **
- Salmon jumping out of a river, two black bears, a boy and girl on horseback ... **

> * I used these topics after learning that some students were being teased for not having the latest fad in shoes. One boy, though he wrote a paragraph on the subject, didn't stop his teasing and, therefore, had to read his second paragraph out loud to his class. That finally ended his teasing.

> ** Students wrote their stories from pictures placed in front of the classroom.

4. Scene Setters To Develop Into Stories: (75-95)

- It's the year 2025. What will you be doing?
- *"The Day I was Swallowed by the Vacuum Cleaner"* by A. Spider. Describe how you feel, what you do, and what happens to you after you are swept up in a vacuum cleaner.
- You are a giraffe. Describe the advantages and disadvantages that you have.

- What would the consequences be if everybody suddenly grew two feet taller?
- Suppose you, like Alice in Wonderland, suddenly shrank so that you were only 12" high. What kinds of things would you do? How would you live?
- Imagine that you are a television anchor person and you are interviewing either a famous historical figure or a contemporary one right after an important event: Lincoln after the Battle of Gettysburg; an eyewitness to the shooting of John Kennedy; Cal Ripkin right after his induction into the Baseball Hall of Fame; an astronaut right after she returns from space; someone else of your choosing.
- Describe what happens when you switch places for one week with someone else: A rock star, an Olympic medalist, an astronaut, a soldier back from war, the President of the United States, or someone else of your choosing.
- You are a cat or dog, a hamster or a fish. Write a letter to your owner who has been away for a week.
- You are a gym shoe. Describe your life.
- If your ruler were a magic wand, what would you do with it?
- There I stood; the dragon was coming right at me....
- There I was, my first time on a babysitting job
- Choose a letter of the alphabet that you like, either for the way it looks when written or it pleases you to start with that letter. As you write, use many words that start with, or use, the letter you have chosen. (Q is quaint and quick to make...; an S is surely something...; Rs are arrogant and refined...)
- You discover an old trunk in your attic. What is in it and to whom did the items belong?
- Find a picture in a magazine of a room you especially like. Paste it at the top of your paper. How does this room make you feel? What you would do in that room if it were in your house?
- I woke up suddenly last night when I heard footsteps outside my door.
- Write a news report in which you describe an imaginary event, either one that could be true like a large fire downtown or one that is fictional, such as describing visitors from another planet or a group of dinosaurs you discovered living in an unexplored area of Africa.
- Give a report on what you saw and what you did when you found yourself suddenly taken by a U.F.O. to an unknown planet where you spent a day. How can you prove you were there?

Probe and Shed Light

- You are a peach. Describe how you look, what you think about, what your hopes are, what your future looks like, etc.
- You are a leaf. It is autumn. You have been blown off your tree and now you are being blown toward a highway. What happens to you?

5. Develop One of These Sayings Into A Story, Or Use It To Write A Fable With The Saying As Your Moral (95-101)

- "A stitch in time saves nine." (Being prepared may save much work later.)
- "Don't count your chickens before they are hatched." (Don't plan on something happening before it actually does.)
- "Don't put all your eggs in one basket." (Don't depend entirely on one idea or one occurrence and don't pin your hopes on just one thing.)
- "Look before you leap." (Be careful before you get involved with something.)
- "The grass is always greener on the other side of the fence." (Some people are never satisfied with what they have; other people's possessions or lives seem better; they show greediness.)
- "A watched pot never boils." (When you're waiting for something you want to happen, it seems that it will never take place.)
- "Into each life some rain must fall, some days must be dark and dreary." Henry Wadsworth Longfellow

6. PLUS 1 & 2

Plus I: Look For Inviting Rooms and interesting scenes by going through magazines, large calendars, etc. Ask your children to write what they would do in such a room or in the scene or what they think those in the scene are saying. Scour second-hand bookstores for old issues of magazines, especially *Saturday Evening Posts*, some of which cry out for a story! Look especially for Norman Rockwell paintings, or find some online, as

Probe and Shed Light

they almost always convey a story. Cut out or make a copy of the picture and post it where the children can see it.

At the first of each month, go to http://www.readwritethink.org/calendar/. Have children write a paragraph about the people or events that are portrayed. Use the historical information and linked suggestions for activities related to certain dates for more research and writing.

Plus 2: Arrays of Color: A reading, writing, and researching exercise

Provide a blank paper or poster board for your children, so that by themselves, with a partner or group can display examples they find. Gather garden catalogs that show every sort of plant, vegetable, herb, etc.; grocery store flyers showing produce; magazines likely to advertise jewelry; jewelry store brochures that show green gems (emeralds, jade, malachite, beryl), and turn to the Internet for more. Or, have your students draw and color their own pictures.

Take your students to a paint store where they can select strips of green paint samples and assess the names given each shade. Visit a travel agency in quest of a photo of Ireland showing why it is called the Emerald Isle. Can they create a picture of Dorothy's Emerald City? If your family enjoys this lesson, you can download similar ones for blue and red colors by going to the link below.

Greens: In gems, nature, clothing, pigments (think fruits, birds' feathers, vegetables, minerals; products of nature) whose names indicate "green", along with a plethora of idioms, such as green horn, green-eyed monster, greenhouse effect, green thumb...). Well, you get the picture. All the colors provide opportunities for dynamic discussions, creative writing, and special projects. For a complete lesson on greens and other colors, go to www.wordwebvocabulary.com/downloads.html#tests
http://www.uncp.edu/home/canada/work/allam/general/glossary.htm
http://www.infoplease.com/ipa/A0934952.html

F: ENGLISH LANGUAGE ENRICHMENT

Children's Favorite Classic Poems

"Poetry is the journal of the sea animal living on land, wanting to fly in the air. Poetry is a search for syllables to shoot at the barriers of the unknown and the unknowable. Poetry is a phantom script telling how rainbows are made and why they go away."

Carl Sandburg

Want to challenge your students while slipping in big doses of cultural literacy and reinforcing basic skills? Use this fresh approach to enrich current studies, to extend students' literacy, and to supply impetus for students to recite poetry, to master difficult spelling words, and whatever else you want your students to accomplish but which students might say, "That's too hard!" If you teach a group of at least ten children, allow those who feel uncomfortable reciting in front of others to listen to others' recitations. They'll absorb them, anyway.

If children designate some challenges as being "too hard," add the promise of a small reward, and you'll receive an positive response.

Memorizing poems not only provides an outlet for the academic energies of the students who attempt them but also increases their memorization skills. Furthermore, they allow otherwise insecure children to perform in front of their peers in a way that differs immeasurably from the regular classroom format. The poems provide opportunities to reinforce students' knowledge of the effects of sound (alliteration, onomatopoeia, or rhyme schemes) and those of personification, metaphor, simile, and hyperbole.

Encourage everyone to try at least one challenge each month. Set aside the same time each week (Friday afternoon?) and give four opportunities for children to succeed. Elementary school children highly prize badges such as those you can make by using materials supplied with a Badge-a-Minit˙ kit. Many children like to wear a "sash" in the manner of Boy/Girl Scouts to which they attach their badges.

Choose age-appropriate selections for your scholars. Young children may enjoy writing and illustrating many of these. For long selections, allow students to divide up stanzas, each saying at least one.

FLYING KITE: Frank Sherman

I often sit and wish that I
Could be a kite up in the sky,
And ride upon the breeze, and go
Whatever way it chanced to blow.
Then I could look beyond the town,
And see the river winding down,
And follow all the ships that sail
Like me before the merry gale,
Until at last with them I came
To some place with a foreign name.

THE SWALLOW: Ogden Nash

Swallow, swallow, swooping free,
Do you not remember me?
I think last spring that it was you
Who tumbled down the sooty flue
With wobbly wings and gaping face,
A fledgling in the fireplace.

Remember how I nursed and fed you,
And then into the air I sped you?
How I wish that you would try
To take me with you as you fly.

WE LIKE MARCH: Emily Dickinson

We like March - his shoes are Purple.
He is new and high.
Makes he Mud for Dog and Peddler.
Makes he Forests Dry.
Knows the Adders' tongue his coming
And begets her spot.
Stands the Sun so close and mighty
That our Minds are hot.
News is he of all the others
Bold it were to die
With the Blue Birds buccaneering
On his British sky.

MARCH: Emily Dickinson

Dear March, come in!
How glad I am!
I looked for you before.
Put down your hat—
You must have walked—
How out of breath you are!
Dear March, how are you?
And the rest?
Did you leave Nature well?
Oh, March, come right upstairs with me.
I have so much to tell.

THE MIDNIGHT RIDE OF PAUL REVERE
By Henry Wadsworth Longfellow

Listen my children and you shall hear
Of the midnight ride of Paul Revere.
Twas the eighteenth of April in '75;
Hardly a man is now alive
Who remembers that famous day and year.

He said to his friends "If the British march
By land or sea from the town tonight,
Hang a lantern aloft in the belfry arch
Of the North Church tower as a signal light,--
One if by land, and two if by sea;
And I on the opposite shore will be,
Ready to ride and spread the alarm
Through every Middlesex village and farm,
For the country folk to be up and to arm."

Read the rest of this poem to learn the whole story.
http://www.nationalcenter.org/PaulRevere'sRide.html

**This poem would make a great class project with different children, either as
a group or by themselves, reciting each of the 13 verses.**

APRIL: Sara Teasdale

The roofs are shining from the rain,
The sparrows twitter as they fly;
And with a windy April grace
The little clouds go by.

Yet the backyards are bare and brown
With only one unchanging tree -
I could not be so sure of Spring
Save that it sings in me.

RAIN: Robert Louis Stevenson

The rain is falling all around,
 It falls on field and tree,
It rains on the umbrellas here,
And on the ships at sea.

APRIL RAIN SONG: Langston Hughes

Let the rain kiss you.
Let the rain beat upon your
    head with silver liquid drops.
Let the rain sing you a lullaby.

The rain makes still pools on the sidewalk.
The rain makes running pools in the gutter.
The rain plays a little sleep-song on our roof at night -
And I love the rain.

SONG: Robert Browning

The year's at the spring
And day's at the morn;
Morning's at seven;
The hillside's dew-pearled;
The lark's on the wing;
The snail's on the thorn;
God's in his heaven -
All's right with the world.

THE ARROW AND THE SONG:
Henry Wadsworth Longfellow

I shot an arrow into the air;
It fell to earth, I know not where;
For so swiftly it flew, the sight
Could not follow it in its flight.

I breathed a song into the air;
It fell to earth, I know not where;
For who has sight so keen and strong,
That it can follow the flight of song?

Long, long afterward, in an oak
I found the arrow, still unbroke;
And the song, from beginning to end,
I found again in the heart of a friend.

THE SWING: Robert Louis Stevenson

How do you like to go up in a swing,
    Up in the air so blue?
Oh, I do think it is the pleasantest thing
    Ever a child can do!

Up in the air and over the wall,
    Till I can see so wide,
Rivers and trees and cattle and all
    Over the countryside -

Till I look down on the garden green,
    Down on the roof so brown -
    Up in the air I go flying again,
Up in the air and down!

WHO HAS SEEN THE WIND?: Christina Rossetti

Who has seen the wind?
Neither I nor you;
But when the leaves hang trembling,
The wind is passing through.

Who has seen the wind?
Neither you nor I;
But when the trees bow down their heads,
The wind is passing by.

THE MOON'S THE NORTH WIND'S COOKY
Vachel Lindsay

The Moon's the North Wind's cooky.
He bites it day by day,
Until there's but a rim of scraps
That crumble all away.
The South Wind is a baker.
He kneads clouds in his den,
And bakes a crisp new moon that ...
greedy North . . Wind .. eats .. again!

THE WIND: Robert Louis Stevenson

I saw you toss the kites on high
And blow the birds about the sky;
And all around I heard you pass,
Like ladies' skirts across the grass -
    O wind, a-blowing all day long,
    O wind, that sings so loud a song!

I saw the different things you did,
But always you yourself you hid.
I felt you push, I heard you call,
I could not see yourself at all -
    O wind, a-blowing all day long,
    O wind, that sings so loud a song!

O you that are so strong and cold,
O blower, are you young or old?
Are you a beast of field and tree,
Or just a stronger child than me?
O wind, a-blowing all day long,
O wind, that sings so loud a song!

WINDY NIGHT: Robert Louis Stevenson

Whenever the moon and stars are set,
    Whenever the wind is high,
All night long in the dark and wet,
    A man goes riding by.
Late in the night when the fires are out,
Why does he gallop and gallop about?

Whenever the trees are crying aloud,
    And ships are tossed at sea,
By, on the highway, low and loud,
    By at the gallop goes he.
By at the gallop he goes, and then
By he comes back at the gallop again.

SOMETHING TOLD THE WILD GEESE
Rachel Field

Something told the wild geese
It was time to go.
Though the fields lay golden
Something whispered, "Snow."
Leaves were green and stirring
Berries, luster-glossed,
But beneath warm feathers
Something cautioned, "Frost."

All the sagging orchards
Steamed with amber spice,
But each wild breast stiffened
At remembered ice.
Something told the wild geese
It was time to fly -
Summer sun was on their wings,
Winter in their cry.

MY SHADOW: Robert Louis Stevenson

I have a little shadow that goes in
and out with me.
And what can be the use of him is
more than I can see.
He is very, very like me from the
heels up to the head;
And I see him jump before me, when
I jump into my bed.

The funniest thing about him is the
way he likes to grow -
  Not at all like proper children,
which is always very slow;
For he sometimes shoots up taller
like an India-rubber ball,
And he sometimes gets so little
that there's none of him at all.

He hasn't got a notion of how
children ought to play,
And can only make a fool of me in
every sort of way.
He stays so close beside me, he's
a coward you can see;
I'd think shame to stick to nursie
as that shadow sticks to me!

One morning, very early, before
the sun was up,
I rose and found the shining dew
on every buttercup;
But my lazy little shadow, like an
arrant sleepy-head,
Had stayed at home behind me and
was fast asleep in bed.

THE FLAG GOES BY: Henry Holcomb Bennett

HATS off!

Along the street there comes
A blare of bugles, a ruffle of drums,
A flash of color beneath the sky:
Hats off!
The flag is passing by!

Blue and crimson and white it shines,
Over the steel-tipped, ordered lines.
Hats off!
The colors before us fly;
But more than the flag is passing by.

Sea-fights and land-fights, grim and great,
Fought to make and to save the State:
Weary marches and sinking ships;
Cheers of victory on dying lips;

Days of plenty and years of peace;
March of a strong land's swift increase;
Equal justice, right and law,
Stately honor and reverend awe;

Sign of a nation, great and strong
To ward her people from foreign wrong:
Pride and glory and honor,—all
Live in the colors to stand or fall.

Hats off!
Along the street there comes
A blare of bugles, a ruffle of drums;
And loyal hearts are beating high:
Hats off!
The flag is passing by!

THE QUALITY OF MERCY: William Shakespeare
From *The Merchant of Venice, Act 4 scene I*

The quality of mercy is not strain'd,
It droppeth as the gentle rain from heaven
Upon the place beneath. It is twice blest:
It blesseth him that gives and him that takes.
'T is mightiest in the mightiest: it becomes
The throned monarch better than his crown;
His sceptre shows the force of temporal power,
The attribute to awe and majesty,
Wherein doth sit the dread and fear of kings;
But mercy is above this sceptred sway,
It is enthroned in the hearts of kings,
It is an attribute to God himself;
And earthly power doth then show likest God's,
When mercy seasons justice. Therefore, Jew,
Though justice be thy plea, consider this,
That in the course of justice none of us
Should see salvation: we do pray for mercy;
And that same prayer doth teach us all to render
The deeds of mercy.

THE CHARGE OF THE LIGHT BRIGADE:
Alfred, Lord Tennyson

This poem memorializes the disastrous charge of British
cavalry led by Lord Cardigan against Russian forces in the
Battle of Balaclava: October 25, 1854

Half a league half a league,
Half a league onward,
All in the valley of Death
Rode the six hundred:
'Forward, the Light Brigade!
Charge for the guns' he said:
Into the valley of Death
Rode the six hundred.

'Forward, the Light Brigade!'
Was there a man dismay'd?
Not tho' the soldier knew
Some one had blunder'd:
Theirs not to make reply,
Theirs not to reason why,
Theirs but to do & die,
Into the valley of Death
Rode the six hundred.

Cannon to right of them,
Cannon to left of them,
Cannon in front of them
Volley'd & thunder'd;
Storm'd at with shot and shell,
Boldly they rode and well,
Into the jaws of Death,
Into the mouth of Hell
Rode the six hundred.

Flash'd all their sabres bare,
Flash'd as they turn'd in air
Sabring the gunners there,
Charging an army while
All the world wonder'd:
Plunged in the battery-smoke
Right thro' the line they broke;
Cossack & Russian
Reel'd from the sabre-stroke,
Shatter'd & sunder'd.
Then they rode back, but not
Not the six hundred.

Cannon to right of them,
Cannon to left of them,
Cannon behind them
Volley'd and thunder'd;
Storm'd at with shot and shell,
While horse & hero fell,
They that had fought so well
Came thro' the jaws of Death,
Back from the mouth of Hell,
All that was left of them,
Left of six hundred.

When can their glory fade?
O the wild charge they made!
All the world wonder'd.
Honour the charge they made!
Honour the Light Brigade,
Noble six hundred!

The story behind *The Charge Of The Light Brigade*
http://www.victorianweb.org/history/crimea/chargelb.html

RECESSIONAL: Rudyard Kipling

God of our fathers, known of old--
Lord of our far-flung battle line
Beneath whose awful hand we hold
Dominion over palm and pine--
Lord God of Hosts, be with us yet,
Lest we forget - lest we forget!

The tumult and the shouting dies;
The captains and the kings depart:
Still stands Thine ancient sacrifice,
An humble and a contrite heart.
Lord God of Hosts, be with us yet,
Lest we forget - lest we forget!

Far-called, our navies melt away
On dune and headland sinks the fire:
Lo, all our pomp of yesterday
Is one with Nineveh and Tyre!
Judge of the Nations, spare us yet,
Lest we forget - lest we forget!

If, drunk with sight of power, we loose
Wild tongues that have not Thee in awe
Such boasting as the Gentiles use
Or lesser breeds without the law
Lord God of Hosts, be with us yet,
Lest we forget - lest we forget!

For heathen heart that puts her trust
In reeking tube and iron shard
All valiant dust that builds on dust,
And guarding, calls not Thee to guard
For frantic boast and foolish word,
Thy mercy on Thy people, Lord!

RING OUT, WILD BELLS: Alfred, Lord Tennyson;

Ring out, wild bells, to the wild sky,
The flying cloud, the frosty light:
The year is dying in the night--
Ring out, wild bells, and let him die.

Ring out the old, ring in the new--,
Ring happy bells, across the snow:
The year is going, let him go;
Ring out the false, ring in the true.

Ring out the grief that saps the mind,
For those that here we see no more;
Ring out the feud of rich and poor,
Ring in redress to all mankind.

Ring out a slowly dying cause,
And ancient forms of party strife;
Ring in the nobler modes of life,
With sweeter manners, purer laws.

Ring out the want, the care, the sin,
The faithless coldness of the times;
Ring out, ring out my mournful rhymes,
But ring the fuller minstrel in.

Ring out false pride in place and blood,
The civic slander and the spite;
Ring in the love of truth and right,
Ring in the common love of good.

Ring out old shapes of foul disease,
Ring out the narrowing lust of gold;
Ring out the thousand wars of old,
Ring in the thousand years of peace.

Ring in the valiant man and free,
The larger heart, the kindlier hand;
Ring out the darkness of the land--
Ring in the Christ that is to be.

UNTITLED: by Archibald MacLeish
(written on the occasion of the first moon landing)

"Three days and three nights we journeyed,
steered by farthest stars, climbed outward,
crossed the invisible tide-rip where
the floating dust falls one way or the other
 in the void between
followed that other down, encountered
cold, faced death -
unfathomable emptiness.

"Then, the fourth day evening,
we descended,
made fast, set foot at dawn upon your beaches,
sifted between our fingers
your cold sand."

DAFFODILS: William Wordsworth

I wander'd lonely as a cloud
That floats on high o'er vales and hills,
When all at once I saw a crowd,
A host, of golden daffodils;
Beside the lake, beneath the trees,
Fluttering and dancing in the breeze.

Continuous as the stars that shine
And twinkle on the Milky Way,
They stretch'd in never-ending line
 Along the margin of a bay;
Ten thousand saw I at a glance,
Tossing their heads in sprightly dance.

The waves beside them danced; but they
Out-did the sparkling waves in glee;
A poet could not but be gay,
In such a jocund company;
I gazed - and gazed - but little thought
What wealth the show to me had brought.

For oft, when on my couch I lie
In vacant or in pensive mood,
They flash upon that inward eye
Which is the bliss of solitude;
And then my heart with pleasure fills,
And dances with the daffodils.

STOPPING BY WOODS ON A SNOWY EVENING:
Robert Frost

Whose woods these are I think I know.
His house is in the village though;
He will not see me stopping here
To watch his woods fill up with snow.

The little horse must think it queer
To stop without a farmhouse near
Between the woods and frozen lake
The darkest evening of the year.

He gives his harness bells a shake
To ask if there is some mistake.
The only other sound's the sweep
Of easy wind and downy flake.

The woods are lovely, dark and deep,
But I have promises to keep,
And miles to go before I sleep,
And miles to go before I sleep.

FIRE AND ICE: Robert Frost

Some say the world will end in fire,
Some say in ice.
From what I've tasted of desire
I hold with those who favor fire.
But if it had to perish twice,
I think I know enough of hate
To know that for destruction ice
Is also great
And would suffice.

ROADWAYS: John Masefield

One road leads to London.
One road runs to Wales.
My road leads me seawards
To the white dipping sails.

One road leads to the river,
As it goes singing slow;
My road leads to shipping
Where the bronzed sailors go.

Leads me, lures me, calls me
To salt green tossing sea;
A road without earth's road dust
Is the right road for me.

A wet road heaving, shining
And wild with seagull's cries.
A mad salt sea-wind blowing
The salt sea in my eyes.

My road calls me, lures me
West, east, south, and north;
Most roads lead me homewards.
My road leads me forth.

INSCRIPTION ON THE STATUE OF LIBERTY:
Emma Lazarus

Give me your tired, your poor,
Your huddled masses yearning
    to breathe free,
The wretched refuse of your teeming shore,
Send these, the homeless,
tempest-tossed, to me;
I lift my lamp beside the golden door.

AN INTRODUCTION TO DOGS: Ogden Nash
(Consider having each verse recited by a different student.)

The dog is man's best friend.
He has a tail on one end.
Up in front he has teeth.
And four legs underneath.

Dogs like to bark.
They like it best after dark.
They not only frighten prowlers away
But also hold the sandman at bay.

A dog that is indoors
To be let out implores.
You let him out and what then?
He wants back in again.

Dogs display reluctance and wrath
If you try to give them a bath.
They bury bones in hideaways
And half the time they trot sideaways.

They cheer up people who are frowning,
And rescue people who are drowning.
They also track mud on beds,
And chew people's clothes to shreds.

Dogs in the country have fun.
They run and run and run.
But in the city this species
Is dragged around on leashes.

*(**Make this last verse a chorus.**)*
Dogs are upright as a steeple
And much more loyal than people.

PREAMBLE TO THE CONSTITUTION

WE THE PEOPLE of the United States,
in order to form a more perfect Union,
establish Justice, insure domestic tranquility,
provide for the common Defense,
promote the general Welfare,
and secure the Blessings of Liberty
to ourselves and our Posterity,
DO ordain and establish this
Constitution for the United States of America

IF: Rudyard Kipling

If you can keep your head when all about you
Are losing theirs and blaming it on you,
If you can trust yourself when all men doubt you
But make allowance for their doubting too,
If you can wait and not be tired by waiting,
Or being lied about, don't deal in lies,
Or being hated, don't give way to hating,
And yet don't look too good, nor talk too wise;

If you can dream - and not make dreams your master,
If you can think - and not make thoughts your aim;
If you can meet with Triumph and Disaster
And treat those two impostors just the same;
If you can bear to hear the truth you've spoken
Twisted by knaves to make a trap for fools,
Or watch the things you gave your life to, broken,
And stoop and build 'em up with worn-out tools:

If you can make one heap of all your winnings
And risk it all on one turn of pitch-and-toss,
And lose, and start again at your beginnings
And never breathe a word about your loss;
If you can force your heart and nerve and sinew
To serve your turn long after they are gone,
And so hold on when there is nothing in you
Except the will which says to them: "Hold on!"

Probe and Shed Light

THE LADY OF SHALOTT: Alfred, Lord Tennyson

On either side the river lie
Long fields of barley and of rye,
That clothe the wold and meet the sky;
And through the field the road run by
To many-tower'd Camelot;
And up and down the people go,
Gazing where the lilies blow
Round an island there below,
The island of Shalott.

Willows whiten, aspens quiver,
Little breezes dusk and shiver
Through the wave that runs for ever
By the island in the river
Flowing down to Camelot.
Four grey walls, and four grey towers,
Overlook a space of flowers,
And the silent isle imbowers
The Lady of Shalott.

By the margin, willow veil'd,
Slide the heavy barges trail'd
By slow horses; and unhail'd
The shallop flitteth silken-sail'd
Skimming down to Camelot:
But who hath seen her wave her hand?
Or at the casement seen her stand?
Or is she known in all the land,
The Lady of Shalott?
Only reapers, reaping early,
In among the bearded barley
Hear a song that echoes cheerly
From the river winding clearly;
Down to tower'd Camelot;
And by the moon the reaper weary,
Piling sheaves in uplands airy,
Listening, whispers, " 'Tis the fairy
The Lady of Shalott."
(15 more stanzas)

VI: FIGURATIVELY SPEAKING

"We don't just borrow words; on occasion, English has pursued other languages down alleyways to beat them unconscious and riffle their pockets for new vocabulary."
James D. Nicoll

A. METAPHORS: Figures of speech that make direct comparisons between seemingly unrelated subjects. We replace "normal" words to make comparisons that show how two things that are not alike in most ways are similar in one important way. Unlike similes, (below) that use "as" or "like" to make a comparison, metaphors state that something *is* something else. Create your own metaphors when you write.

1. Examples

   a. "All the world's a stage, And all the men and women merely players; They have their exits and their entrances." William Shakespeare: *As You Like It*
   b. My spirits are higher than a kite.
   c. People who ride bicycles or drive cars so as to prevent others from passing them are road hogs.
   d. A constant source of irritation is a **thorn in one's side**: This expression appears twice in the Bible. In Judges 2:3 it is enemies that *"shall be as thorns in your sides;"* in II Corinthians 12:7 Paul says his infirmities are *"given to me a thorn in the flesh."* Explain: Sometimes, being a friend means being a thorn in one's side. Turkey (the country) is thought to be a thorn in the side of a Western accord. Why?
   e. Joe borrows money from Jim in order to give Mary the money he owes her. We call this **Robbing Peter to pay Paul**. (This is not a biblical saying.)
   f. Today's wind was _____

Probe and Shed Light

2. POETIC METAPHOR: A Group Project

"TREES"
by Joyce Kilmer

I think that I shall never see
A poem lovely as a tree.
A tree that looks at God all day,
And lifts her leafy arms to pray.
A tree that may in Summer wear
A nest of robins in her hair;
Upon whose bosom snow has lain;
Who intimately lives with rain,
Poems are made by fools like me,
But only God can make a tree.

Joyce Kilmer's poem "Trees" can provide many insights for students. As an adult, I believed that there was a much better way to connect children to this poem than that my fifth grade teacher used by having us memorize it. Not only did it have little meaning for me (and I'm sure for some of my classmates, as well), we also thought the poem was silly. Many years later, as I began to notice and appreciate different types of trees, I remembered Mr. Kilmer's poem and finally understood its meaning.

Because I would like youngsters to appreciate this poem—not just for the moment but for the future as well—I feel they should study a variety of trees <u>before</u> reading the poem. Take/send your children to scour the neighborhood (regardless of the season) and have each choose a tree of his or her liking, then sketch or take pictures of it. Indoors, have students expand their pictures or drawings to a full-fledged piece of art. If going outdoors to sketch a tree is unlikely where you live, then children can download those they like best from the Google˚ images site or at: <u>http://www.autumnridgenursery.com/</u>.

Each should explain his reason(s) for choosing that particular tree. This activity is bound to further the student's understanding of the poem. Repeat these in other seasons.

To extend this project, older students can research how trees have held sacred meanings throughout the ages, as in *The Tree of Knowledge of Good and Evil* mentioned in the Book of Genesis and *The Axis Mundi*, or world axis, which now takes the form of a tree in Christian mythology. Students can also draw a tree showing their families' genealogies.

Discuss the proverb below with your students. How can we relate it to Henry Abbey's poem?

Greek Proverb

"A society grows great when old men plant trees whose shade they know they shall never sit in."

"WHAT DO WE PLANT WHEN WE PLANT A TREE?"
Henry Abbey

What do we plant when we plant the tree?
We plant the ship which will cross the sea.
We plant the mast to carry the sails,
We plant the planks to withstand the gales,
The keel, the keelson, the beam, and knee.
We plant the ship when we plant the tree.

What do we plant when we plant the tree?
We plant the house for you and me.
We plant the rafters, the shingles, the floors,
We plant the studding, the lath, the doors.
The beams and siding, all parts that be.
We plant the house when we plant the tree.

What do we plant when we plant the tree?
A thousand things that we daily see.
We plant the spire that out-towers the crag,
We plant the shade from the hot sun free.
We plant all these things when we plant the tree.

REFERENCES

http://www.serve.com/hecht/words/fos.htm
http://www.angelfire.com/ct2/evenski/poetry/figuresofspeech.html
http://www.rhlschool.com/eng3n26.htm
http://owl.english.purdue.edu/handouts/general/gl_metaphor.html
http://grammar.about.com/od/mo/g/metaphorterm.htm

B. **ADAGE**: A short but memorable saying that holds some important fact or experience, considered true by many, is a good way to keep the brain active. Ask your students for at least one example for each of these. Here's one I made up: *"An adage a day keeps children bright and thoughtful!"*

1. Actions speak louder than words.
2. The grass is greener on the other side of the fence.
3. Good fences make good neighbors.
4. Still waters run deep.
5. Tomorrow never comes.
6. He who hesitates is lost.
7. Haste makes waste.
8. A miss is as good as a mile.
9. Waste not, want not.
10. Early to bed, early to rise, makes a man healthy, wealthy, and wise.
11. Ignorance is bliss.
12. The best things in life are free.
13. A quiet conscience sleeps in thunder.
14. Self-respect is that cornerstone of all virtue.
15. God gives every bird its food, but he does not throw it into the nest.
16. He who loses his conscience has nothing left that is worth keeping.
17. Even a fool is counted wise when he holds his peace. Proverbs
18. Don't judge a book by its cover.
19. Don't look a gift horse in the mouth.
20. Smile and the whole world smiles with you.

How about having your children/students finish these lines in what they think is an appropriate manner? (Expect a lot of humor before getting serious!)

If at first you don't succeed _____ (Standard answer: try, try again.)

When it rains, it _____ (Standard answer: it pours.)

Look before_____(Standard answer: you leap.)

A watched pot _____ (Standard answer: never boils.)

For many more adages, go to the Appendix.

C. ALLITERATION: The repetition of the same consonant sound or of different vowel sounds at the beginning of words or in stressed syllables

1. The terrific terrier turned a trick.

2. Mothers mastermind millions of miracles.

3. Pria, the pony, pranced perfectly for the audience.

4. **Dancing Dolphins** by Paul McCann
   Those tidal thoroughbreds tango through the turquoise tide.
   Their taut tails thrashing they twist in tribute to the titans.
   They twirl through the trek
   tumbling towards the tide.
   Throwing themselves towards those theatrical thespians.

5. Encourage students to write one or more alliterations of their own.

D. ANALOGY: Comparison expressing similarity in some respects between two things that are otherwise dissimilar. Sometimes the two things are the same in some way; other times they are opposites: *An analogy between the heart and a pump.* Similarity or comparability: *I see no analogy between your problem and mine.*

1. "My Love is Like a Red, Red Rose." A 1794 song by Robert Burns

2. Some write analogies this way—**water : liquid : : ice : solid**— and read as—water is to liquid as ice is to solid.

3. Spring : fall : : summer: _____.

4. Pencil is to write as brush is to paint.

5. _____ : _____ : : _____ _____

We can state that something is analogous to something else. For example, being housebound by the deep snow is **analogous** to being in jail.

http://www.funtrivia.com/playquiz/quiz1595191244b90.html
http://www.gamequarium.com/readquarium/analogies.html

E. ANTONYM: A word that has the opposite meaning of another. Have students fill in the blanks with words that seem fit.

1. hot—cold
2. tall—short
3. interesting—boring
4. brave—_____
5. whispered—_____
6. _____— sister
7. Ask students to create 10 more of their own.

F. APHORISM: A concise and often witty statement of wisdom or opinion; a terse saying embodying a general truth, or astute observation; brief statement of a principle, an instructive saying. Discuss these with your students; ask them for examples that fit the aphorism.

1. A little consideration, a little thought for others, makes all the difference. **Joan Powers**
2. A single death is a tragedy, a million deaths is statistics. **Josef Stalin**
3. Better to light a candle than to curse the darkness. **Unknown**
4. Conscience is the inner voice that warns us somebody is looking. **Henry Louis Mencken**
5. How far that little candle throws his beams! So shines a good deed in a weary world. **William Shakespeare**
6. If you were arrested for kindness, would there be enough evidence to convict you? **Unknown**
7. Kind words can be short and easy to speak, but their echoes are truly endless. **Mother Teresa**
8. Tact is the ability to describe others as they see themselves. **Abraham Lincoln**
9. Thinking good thoughts is not enough; doing good deeds is not enough; seeing others follow your good examples is enough. **Doug Horton**
10. We owe almost all our knowledge not to those who have agreed, but to those who have differed. **G.C. Colton**
11. Always do right. This will gratify some people and astonish the rest. **Mark Twain**
12. Anger is never without a reason, but seldom with a good one. **Benjamin Franklin**
13 If you tell the truth you don't have to remember anything. **Mark Twain**

14. Never be afraid to try something new. Remember, amateurs built the ark. Professionals built the Titanic. **Unknown**
15. No one can make you feel inferior without your consent. **Eleanor Roosevelt**

http://www.srichinmoypoetry.com/aphorisms http://penn.betatesters.com/wisdom02.htm
http://members.dca.net/leipold/ap_ap.html
http://www.faculty.rsu.edu/~felwell/HomePage/aphorisms.htm

G. **EUPHEMISM (Greek *eu-* well + *phēmē* speech):** Words or phrases designed to disguise or distort their actual meanings with the intention of making something bad sound better. These are a form of "doublespeak." Euphemistically speaking, we might say:

1. Family room instead of TV room
2. Grandma passed on rather than, Grandma died.
3. Downsizing for firing many employees
4. Post-traumatic stress disorder instead World War I's shell shock
5. Physically challenged for handicapped
6. Mentally challenged instead of dumb/stupid
7. Hearing-and-speaking impaired instead of deaf and dumb
8. Speaks up for himself versus loud-mouth
9. He has a chemical dependency rather than, He's an addict/substance abuser.
10. fat vs. amply proportioned
11. building maintenance staff vs. janitor
12. senior citizen vs. old person
13. _____ vs. beggar
14. _____ vs. cheap
15. _____ vs. crippled
16. _____ vs. false teeth

http://grammar.about.com/od/e/g/euphemismterm.htm
http://www.phrases.org.uk/meanings/euphemism.html
http://iteslj.org/Lessons/Alkire-Euphemisms.html

H. HYPERBOLE: A figure of speech in which exaggeration is used for emphasis or effect

1. I could sleep for a year.
2. This book weighs a ton.
3. His voice is louder than a freight train.
4. Her cooking would frighten the hyenas.
5. You're so late that I feel as though I've been waiting here for 100 years!

I. IDIOM AND IDIOMATIC EXPRESSION: A common saying that only native language speakers might understand

1. A penny saved is a penny earned. Example _____
2. It was a toss up. Example _____
3. You're adding fuel to the fire. Example _____
4. She's the apple of his eye. Example _____
5. Have you got an ax to grind? Example _____

For more, go to: http://idioms.thefreedictionary.com/

J. LITERARY ALLUSION: A brief reference, explicit or indirect, to a person, place or event, or to another literary work or passage. Students should research and explain each and try to use at least one of these when writing a story.

1. He cried crocodile (false) tears.
2. He made bricks without straw (He performed a task without basic tools or material.)
3. We decided to bury the hatchet. (We made peace.)
4. He decided he'd better cross the Rubicon. (An irrevocable decisive step.)
5. To sow dragons' teeth: To follow policies that will lead to war

Research and explain the following:

6. He took the lion's share of the credit.
7. She was assigned a Herculean task.
8. It was really a Cinderella story.
9. He's a scrooge!
10. He has the Midas touch.

Answers to the next five are in the Appendix.

11. To cry wolf:
    a. To frighten by a ruse
    b. To give alarm without occasion
    c. To claim aggression while one attacks
12. A Simon Legree
    a. A cruel taskmaster
    b. A mean old man
    c. A fiendish experience
13. To tilt at windmills
    a. To petition the government
    b. To fight imaginary enemies
    c. To attempt the useless
14. A pig in a poke
    a. A great bargain
    b. Something whose true value is unknown
    c. A quick mind
15. To run with the hare and hunt with the hounds
    a. To hesitate
    b. To keep in favor with both parties to an argument
    c. To do a job thoroughly

Read Lemony Snicket stories for more of these allusions: http://www. lemonysnicket.com/

K. ONOMATOPOEIA: Use of words that imitate the sounds associated with the actions or objects to which they refer.

1. The leaves **whispered** as the rain fell softly.
2. She put a real **ding** in the pot's side.
3. The book **clattered** to the floor, its pages **fluttering** in the breeze.
4. The chair **screeched** as it was dragged across the floor.
5. The candle went **poof!** as the breeze grew stronger.

L. OXYMORON (plural: oxymora):   A literary figure of speech usually composed of a combination of contradictory words (often within a sentence).

"I can resist everything but temptation."
Mark Twain

1.   That was a **pretty ugly** statement.
2.   The meat had **freezer burn**.
3.   He is a **student teacher**.
4.   I showed my son **tough love**.
5.   He served in **peace force.**

M. PERSONIFICATION: The representation of an inanimate object or concept as if it had human qualities

"Forests are the lungs of our land, purifying the air
and giving fresh strength to our people."
Franklin D. Roosevelt

1.   Wisdom **calls aloud** in the street.
2.   Fear **knocked** on the door. Faith **answered**. There was no one there.
3.   The lightning **lashed out** with anger.
4.   The trees were **dancing** with the wind.
5.   The wind **whined** and **whistled.**

http://lifestyle.iloveindia.com/lounge/personification-examples-2848.html

N. PROVERB: A simple and concrete saying popularly known and repeated, expressing a truth based on common sense. It relates to everyday circumstances. Ask children for examples; then have them write a short story with the proverb as the topic.
1.   A bad cause requires many words.
2.   A bird in the hand is worth ___ in the bush*
3.   A chain is no stronger than its weakest ___.*
4.   A clear conscience is a soft pillow.
5.   A closed mouth catches no flies.
6.   A fool and his money ___ soon parted.*
7.   A forest is in an acorn.

8. A friend's eye is a good mirror.
9. A new broom sweeps clean, but the old brush knows all the corners.
10. A rumor goes in one ear and out many mouths.
11. A thief believes everybody steals. (Everyone cheats, so why shouldn't I?)
12. All that glitters is ___ gold.*
13. An enemy will agree, but a friend will argue.
14. Anger is as a stone cast into a wasp's nest.
15. Barking dogs seldom bite.
16. Blood is thicker than water.
17. Call on God, but row away from the rocks.
18. Don't count your chickens ___ they are hatched.*
19. Do not look where you fell, but where you slipped.
20. Do not use a hatchet to remove a fly from your friend's forehead.
21. Even a small thorn causes festering.
22. Give a man a fish, and he'll eat for a day. Teach him how to fish and he'll eat forever.
23. Great minds discuss ideas. Average minds discuss events. Small minds discuss people
24. Great talkers are little doers.
25. He who knows nothing, doubts nothing.

*Answers and to read more, go to Appendix.

O. SIMILE: A comparison between two fundamentally unlike things, usually with as or like. Use of similes make writing interesting.

1. I'm as tired **as** a marathon runner.
2. I feel **like** a drooping flower.
3. She threw that ball **as though** she were Babe Ruth.
4. She's **as tall a**s the Statue of Liberty.
5. He's **like** a _____.
6. It traveled as fast as _____.
7. She has a smile **like** _____.
8. It is as dead **as** a _____.
9. This bread is hard **as** _____.
10. This meat is as tough **as** _____.
11. The bump on his head was as large **as** a(n) _____.
12. *Old Chinese Saying*: True friends are like evergreens—you don't know them until winter comes.

Probe and Shed Light

13. My favorite pair of shoes is **like** _____. **Why?** _

    _____.

14. Mike is **like** a _____ when he's painting the house.

P.   **SYNONYM:** A word that has the same meaning as another.

> *"A synonym is a word you use when you can't spell the word*
> *you first thought of."*
> **Burt Bacharach**

1.   peace—repose
2.   tired—weary
3.   modern—new
4.   helpful—_____ *
5.   _____—angry*

*Answers are in the Appendix.

VII. ENGLISH FUN AND GAMES

> *Language is an elaborate and complete display*
> *of the ideas of the culture that speaks it.*
> **Richard Mitchell**

A.   **ANAGRAMS:** An anagram is a word or phrase made by transposing or rearranging the letters of another word or phrase. Let students work with these quite astonishing examples to see whether they can make the transpositions, giving a clue to the number of words in the transposition. Answers to last four are in the Appendix.

1.   dormitory == dirty room
2.   semolina == is no meal
3.   Hitler == the liar
4.   telegraph == great help
5.   the morse code == here come dots
6.   snoozed == dozes on
7.   animosity == is no amity
8.   measured == made sure
9.   problem in Chinese == incomprehensible

10. shrubbery == berry bush
11. upholsterers == restore plush
12. a decimal point =– I'm a dot in place
13. the earthquakes == that queer shake
14. eleven plus two == twelve plus one
15. skin care == irks acne
16. received payment == every cent paid me
17. the eyes == _____ _____
18. Presbyterian == _____ ___ _____
19. Alec Guinness == _____ _____
20. The Earthquakes == _____ _____ _____

B. **HOMONYM HASSLE**S: One of two or more words that have the same sound and often the same spelling but differ in meaning. Can students explain each? Which is a noun, adjective, verb?

1. The bandage was **wound** around the **wound**.
2. The farm was used to **produce produce**.
3. The dump was so full that it had to **refuse** more **refuse**.
4. We must **polish** the **Polish** furniture.
5. He could **lead** if he would get the **lead** out.
6. The soldier decided to **desert** his **dessert** in the **desert**.
7. Since there is no time like the **present**, he thought he should **present** the **present**.
8. A **bass** was painted on the head of the **bass** drum.
9. When shot at, the **dove dove** into the bushes.
10. I did not **object** to the **object**.
11. The insurance for the **invalid** was **invalid**.
12. There was a **row** among the oarsmen about how to **row**.
13. They were too **close** to the door to **close** it.
14. The buck **does** funny things when the **does** are present.
15. A seamstress and a **sewer** fell down into a **sewer** line.
16. To help with planting, the farmer taught his **sow** to **sow**.
17. The **wind** was too strong to **wind** the sail.
18. After a **number** of injections my jaw got **number**.
19. Upon seeing the **tear** in the painting I shed a **tear**.
20. I had to **subject** the **subject** to a series of tests.

Probe and Shed Light

C. **PALINDROMES:** Words, phrases, numbers, or other sequences of units that can be read the same way in either direction. Ignore punctuation.

1. deed, level, redder, noon _____, _____
2. Live not on evil.
3. Yreka bakery (This one's for real in Yreka, CA!)
4. Marge lets Norah see Sharon's telegram.
5. A dog! A panic in a pagoda!
6. A man, a plan, a canal — Panama
7. Madam, I'm Adam (to which she replied) Sir, I'm Iris.
8. Napoleon: Able was I ere I saw Elba.

For history of palindromes and interesting examples, go to: http://en.wikipedia. org/wiki/Palindrome

D. RUBE GOLDBERGS

Use Google® and Wikipedia® to learn about Rube Goldberg and his complex machines designed to accomplish simple tasks. Students will enjoy banding together to create their own "useful" contraptions. http://mousetrapcontraptions. com/

This annual competition simulates the work of Goldberg, a cartoonist known for depicting complex machines designed to accomplish simple tasks. 2008's goal was to assemble a hamburger in at least 20 steps, with at least one precooked patty, two vegetables and two condiments sandwiched between two buns. The 17-member Purdue University Society of Professional Engineers team concocted a 156-step recipe for preparing a hamburger to win the annual national Rube Goldberg Machine Contest.

The team's leader, Drew Wischer, said, "We put 4,000 to 5,000 man-hours into this machine, and all the hard work has been well worth it." The competition rewards machines that most effectively combine creativity with inefficiency and complexity, while completing the assigned task in 20 or more steps. Winning machines must complete two successful runs. Points are deducted if students have to assist the machine once it has started. Judges award points on the creative use of materials, team chemistry, flow of the machine and each machine's theme.

Can you and a group of friends create a Rube Goldberg?

Probe and Shed Light

E. Great Games:

1. **Mind Your Manners**: Board game, ages 2-6, and language cards, ages 3+: Smethport Specialty Co
2. **Loaded Questions**: A getting to know you game: www.loadedquestions.com, plus many more games rated by age;
3. **Go To Press!** A grammar board game, ages 7-12
4. **More games**:
   a. www.learningresources.com
   b. http://www.magneticpoetry.com/
   c. http://www.google.com/Top/Recreation/Humor/Wordplay/
   d. http://www.christianbook.com/Christian/Books/product?item_no=01201&kw=un
   e. game&event=PPCSRC&p=1018818&gclid=COmY_d6mj5ICFQFjHgodlF7m6A
   f. http://www.educationallearninggames.com, including Math Dice
   g. http://www.funtrivia.com/playquiz/quiz1595191244b90.html
   h. http://www.gamequarium.com/readaquarium/analogies.html
   i. http://www.freehangmangames.com/printable-hangman-game/index.html
   j. Game theory from The Teaching Company is sophisticated material for advanced students: http://www.teach12.com/ttcx/CourseDescLong2.aspx?cid=1426

PARENTS: You should check out other sites, as some associated ads are not acceptable for children. Others, I believe, are too scary for young children, while some may require more sophisticated computer software than you have. Actually, nothing beats good old plain paper and pencils, but I'll leave your ***modus operandi*** up to you.

See also Appendix, page 270.

F. **New Planet Memory Jogger**: "My Very Exciting Magic Carpet Just Sailed Under Nine (Palace) Elephants"; or "My Very Excellent Mother Just Sent Us Nine (Perfect) (Cookies)." **M**ercury, **V**enus, **E**arth, **M**ars, **C**eres, **J**uniper, **S**aturn, **U**ranus, **N**eptune (Pluto, Charon, Nix, Hydra, Ceres, Eris, Makemake). Recently, scientists decided that Pluto was not truly a planet but had joined the category of dwarf planet.

Probe and Shed Light

CHAPTER III

▼

MY UNEXPECTED ACQUISITION OF A NEW LANGUAGE

The Awakened Eye Furthers The Art of Seeing

Education that consists in learning things and not the
meaning of them is feeding upon the husks and not the corn.
Mark Twain

"Many an object is not seen, though it falls within the range
of our visual ray, because it does not come within the range
of our intellectual ray, i.e. we are not looking for it."
Henry David Thoreau

An article, "Look at that House" in a 1970's magazine, precipitated one of my most powerful educational epiphanies. The article, in brief, described the author's winning a contest that would take her from her native Minneapolis to New England. Along with a travel itinerary came a booklet, "Old Houses of New England." As she looked through the booklet, she read the captions under photographs that referred to gables, pilasters, pediments, dentils, cornices, and quoins, words that were entirely new to her. As she puzzled over these descriptive terms, she began to see her city neighborhood in a new light, and she was so excited that she managed to get me in the same state.

I read her story more than once and began to look at buildings. I noticed details of the late 18th Century houses in the area where I lived—and in which the school where I was teaching was located—and began to learn the terminology that applied to these buildings' parts — just as she had done! With a bit of study, I gradually began to master the terminology of buildings.

Perhaps you can imagine how my excitement at learning all these new terms spilled over into my classrooms! Naturally, I felt obliged to use my newfound interest and enthusiasm with my students. I called this "vocabulary," little dreaming where it would take me—or how it would pave the way to success for some of my disenchanted students.

Students had been asking for extra credit work, so I began to affix two architectural features and two other words—which today I call either Real World Words˙ or Wicked Words of the Week˙—to their homework. Students immediately enjoyed this, with the result that some of my poorest performing students began achieving at higher levels. I taught it as vocabulary, integrating my first nonstandard subject matter into the classroom. The first assignment I gave students (many of whom were completely indifferent about learning) were two roof styles—gable and gambrel. When asked beforehand to describe their own houses' roofs, none knew the answer (and neither did their parents). The beauty of this choice was that as soon as they went out the school doors, they could see roofs. Not only were my students learning new terminology, they, like me, couldn't get enough of it!

During the next weeks, we mastered gambrel, mansard and hip roofs, and I began requiring students to go through newspapers to acquire pictures of these various styles. Window types were an obvious next choice. Dormer windows provided connections of the root "dorm-" to dormitory, the phrase "dormez-vous" from "Frère Jacques," and the dormouse in *Alice in Wonderland*. When you learn words in this manner, they stay with you for life! The house with the gambrel roof has dormer windows.

Even the most indifferent students came alive when I assigned the tasks of finding and identifying various architectural features in the vicinity of their homes. This meant they became learned in areas beyond their siblings' and parents' knowledge. Their accomplishments produced a positive attitude that spilled over into other areas of their schoolwork. I now hope the same results will snare homeschoolers' interests.

The significance of this type of awakening is the self-assurance it generates. When students meet success in one area, they gain confidence enabling them to achieve in others. After my first class had covered thirty-six architectural terms, we took a walk from the school to downtown. As we went along, we located almost all the elements we had studied, including wonderful ionic columns above a boarded-up movie theater. We got our noses right up to the three most common types of brick bonding, as brick walls were the city's signature architectural design. Every few steps produced an outcry, "Look at that ...! And this! And that over there!"

Once I became awakened to buildings' features, I realized that most of us gaze right past all sorts of objects in our surroundings without actually connecting to them. It reminded me of the time when I bought a new car and suddenly noticed just how many others like it were on the road. I understood that those others had been there all along, but they just had not caught my attention. Just like the architectural features, they had not had any relevancy for me until I'd made my purchase. To be exact, we find only the world we look for.

This was borne out earlier when I became involved in birdwatching, I had never noticed the incessant caroling of robins outside on our lawn or of any other birds in our area. After I became attuned to these daily serenades, I progressed to learning those of other birds. I used a tape of the songs of common birds to test some friends' awareness of these. Invariably, they failed miserably! "I'm so embarrassed;" or, "I should have known that!" were a few remarks, but this was my favorite. "I'm a musician. Why have I never noticed all that song around me?"

Once I recognized this phenomenon of selective blindness, of how we often gloss over what is readily apparent, I cast around for other ways to increase my own and my students' awareness of our observable world, just as Emerson had suggested in the quote above. For instance, why is a television company called "Magnavox?" A camper, "Vagabond?" A mattress, "Posturpedic?" An automobile, "Maverick?" These types of words are all around us but go virtually unquestioned by children and adults alike.

Henry David Thoreau explained this phenomenon in the quote at the top of this chapter, and Ralph Waldo Emerson echoed it by stating, "*People only see what they are prepared to see.*" So, for the most part, we find only the world we look for.

Just think, though, how much easier we all learn and absorb new material when we have our mind and senses aroused to something new, whether we're reading, listening to the radio, riding in a car, or walking outside! Almost everywhere there are stimuli that bear noting. Furthermore, for children, exposure to new images and words at an early age can do much to promote a positive attitude towards all learning.

This type of attention to brand-new knowledge resulted in a first-grader telling a visitor that her dad's doctor was a charlatan and a third grader riding by City Hall exclaiming to her mother, "Look at those Doric columns!" Precocious children, you are probably thinking, but they were not. They were, quite simply, children of average abilities whose eyes and ears were successfully opened through a special vocabulary.

Language development is a natural part of a child's growth. Since words are major tools of thought, we can conclude that the more of them we know, the better our thinking and consciousness of details will be. Furthermore, we have all noticed, I'm sure, that children learn easily almost anything that interests them and that young children are often able to understand and enjoy material traditionally reserved for older ones.

With the up-close knowledge that parents have of their children, they are able to tailor lessons to each one's level of competency and learning styles. One child, for instance, might research a root word such as "chrono-," meaning time, to discover the meaning of chronograms, types of chronometers, and chronographs, synchrony, chronobiology, and the like, while another might be busy working with a chronology of events or with the word chronic (chronic complaining, -pain, -illness, -bad behavior).

A. My Overture to Visual Culture Created Architectural Awareness

"The beginning of wisdom is to call things by their right names."
Chinese Proverb

From prehistoric megaliths, Egyptian temples and shrines, the great buildings of the ancient Greeks and Romans, and on through early Christian and Medieval, Romanesque, Gothic, and Renaissance periods to present-day skyscrapers, there is a language to describe each period's styles of public buildings and houses.

Regardless of its age, every part of a building has a name. Learning each and understanding its purpose is an easy and delightful way to awaken one's eye to the area around us and to gain an understanding of buildings. In America, whether we view a Colonial, Greek Revival, Gothic, Italianate, Renaissance, Second Empire, or Stick style, we will understand the function of its parts, its *raison d'être*. We will recognize each as we do our friends and acquaintances.

A brief summary of buildings' features: showing **Ionic columns, dentils** above columns and inside **pediment**

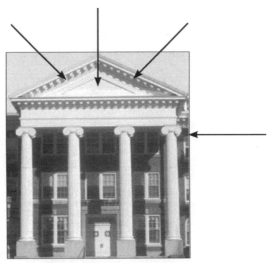

Pediment Arrow at top center
dentils: 2 diagonal arrows
Ionic columns

1. **Roofs:** The four fundamental types: Gable, mansard, hip, gambrel

2. **Uprights:** <u>Columns</u> (round)— Four basic types: Doric, Ionic, Corinthian, composite; <u>pilasters</u> (flat, rectangular): Doric, Ionic, Corinthian, composite; <u>caryatids</u>: Supporting columns sculptured in the form of a draped female figure; <u>atlantes</u>: A standing or kneeling figure of a man used as a supporting column

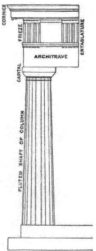

3. **Entablatures** (the superstructure of moldings and bands which lie horizontally above columns and rest on their capitals); <u>architrave</u>: The lowermost part of an entablature in classical architecture that rests directly on top of a column; <u>frieze</u>: A plain or decorated horizontal part of an entablature between the architrave and cornice; <u>cornice</u>: The uppermost part of an entablature; <u>dentils</u>: One of a series of small rectangular blocks projecting like teeth from a

molding or beneath a cornice, <u>modillion</u>: An ornamental bracket used in series under a cornice

4. **Entranceways**: <u>Portico</u>: A porch or walkway with a roof supported by columns, often leading to the entrance of a building; <u>porte-cochère</u>: A carriage entrance; an enclosure over a driveway at the entrance of a building to provide shelter; <u>lintel</u>: The horizontal beam that forms the upper member of a window or door frame and supports the structure above it; <u>arch</u>: A curve with the ends down and the middle up; <u>keystone</u>: The central wedge-shaped stone of an arch that locks its parts together; <u>voussoir</u>: One of the wedge-shaped stones forming the curved parts of an arch or vaulted ceiling; <u>tympanum</u>: The ornamental recessed space or panel enclosed by the cornices of a triangular pediment; <u>spandrel</u>: The space between two arches and a horizontal molding or cornice above them

5. **Windows**: Dormer, Palladian, fanlight, oriel, lunette, rose / wheel;

6. **Decorative Features**: functional: quoins, gargoyles, buttresses, balustrades, cupolas, finials, pediments, niches, quoins; cartouches, cornices, bargeboards, moldings: egg and dart, leaf and tongue, Greek key

7. **Bricks**: The long way of a brick is called a stretcher; the short end is a header. Bricks used in buildings are of three patterns, according to the individual arrangement of the bricks. **Common or stretcher bond** consists of five to seven rows of stretchers with every fifth or seventh row all headers. **English bond** is a row of stretchers alternating with a row headers. **Flemish bond** alternates a row of headers with a row of stretchers. If there are no headers, the bricks are only decorative and are not supporting walls. Take a look at brick buildings in your area. Can you find all three types? Take pictures and write down the location of each. http://www.woodlandsjunior.kent.sch.uk/Homework/houses/walls/

ENGLISH BOND

REFERENCES

Fortunately, there are many materials on this subject, from coloring books to wonderful online sites. After your class has mastered some or all of these terms, be sure to take a walk around your neighborhood, downtown, or to a nearby city. See how many different features you can find. Take pictures! Write down the addresses of your discoveries. Also, encourage your children to notice buildings' characteristic on television and in movies.

Go online, as well, to learn about entertainment architecture. Are there examples where you live? If yes, be sure everyone gets to view them! http://architecture.about.com/cs/20thcentury/g/entertainment.htm?nl=1

Ask your students whether they agree with Johann Wolfgang von Goethe's statement that *"Architecture is frozen music"* or James Stokoe's *"Beauty isn't skin-deep; it's in buildings' bones."* How do they explain their answers?

1. **General**:
   http://www.ontarioarchitecture.com/Styles.html; click on building terms.
   http://architecture.about.com/od/periodsstyles/ig/House-Styles/
   http://www.buffaloah.com/a/DCTNRY/vocab.html, an instructive picture dictionary for help in "translating" this special language:

2. **Coloring books:** http://architecture.about.com/od/teacheraidsk12/tp/coloringbooks.htm
   http://about.pricegrabber.com/search_getprod.php/isbn=9781561382378/search=architecture%20coloring%20book/st=product_tab&mode=about_architecture

3. **Books et al**
   a. **Young Readers:**
      1. How a House Is Built (ISBN: 9780823412327
      2. Houses and Homes (ISBN: 9780688135782
      3. Architects Make Zigzags: Looking at Architecture A to Z
      4. Building a House (ISBN: 0688842917)
      5. Frank Gehry in Pop-up (ISBN: 9781592237906)

   b. **Older Children**
      Under Every Roof: a Kid's Style and Field Guide to the Architecture of American Houses by Patricia Brown ISBN-13: 9780891332145 ISBN: 0891332146

c. Find examples of many architectural features by cutting them from realtors' free adverting pamphlets and pictures in newspapers and magazines.

d. **Many helpful and challenging sites:**
    1. http://architecture.about.com/od/teachersaids/tp/lessonplans.htm
    2. http://architecture.about.com/gi/dynamic/offsite.htm?zi=1/XJ&sdn=architecture&cdn=homegarden&tm=10&f=11&su=p284.9.336.ip_p812.0.336.ip_&tt=3&bt=1&bts=1&zu=http%3A//school.discovery.com/lessonplans/programs/amazingskyscrapers/
    3. http://architecture.about.com/gi/dynamic/offsite.htm?zi=1/XJ&sdn=achitecctureardn=homegarden&tm=71&f=11&su=p284.9.336.ip_p812.0.336.ip_&tt=3&bt=1&bts=1&zu=http%3A//www.cubekc.org/lessons.htm

B. Buildings Lead Me to Word Web Vocabulary

The success I'd had when directing my students' awareness to buildings' elements encouraged me to find other means that would produce the same results. I soon "discovered" other visual aspects of our surroundings, which in future years would become Real World Words©, a part of Word Web Vocabulary©. Many perceptible entities are all around us but go practically unnoticed and, therefore, unquestioned by children and adults alike, such as those below. Present these to your students over time, keeping a list of all they have deciphered.

After discovering that architectural features make good vocabulary lessons, I delved deeper into the broad spectrum of different types of words. After retiring from The Banner School, I wanted to work on an educational project that would keep me busy. As always, when starting a new endeavor, it takes a while to find the perfect format. Once I realized that using a web design would provide a visual array of related words, I was on my way. Each web word indicates its level of difficulty.

However, after creating many webs of roots, prefixes, and suffixes and definitions on the adjacent page, I realized that I had overlooked other types of vocabulary. So, Word Web's second element became the "Real World Word," a variety of words seen or heard but which have no meaning until they are brought into focus, as I indicated above with architectural features, car names, and acronyms. This category also includes foreign words in common English usage, as in laissez-faire, déjà vu, qué sera sera, and idioms: busman's holiday, dumb waiter, elbow grease.

Probe and Shed Light

The third part of Word Web presents standard vocabulary words, not related to the program's two other features. As of this writing, I am marketing three separate volumes. Each has thirty-six lessons, all at the same learning levels. For a complete coverage of Word Web's program, go to http://wordwebvocabulary.com. I hope by the time you read this, you will find me and my thoughts about vocabulary on YouTube, Twitter, and other social sites.

Below is an example from one chapter's web words that I believe homeschoolers will enjoy. Each word is based on *-ette, -et*: French suffixes meaning "small, little." How many more *"-ette"* words can you add to the list? (Hint: There are at least fifty more.)

1.   **–ette**

cassette: In French, *casse* means *case*. A *small*, flat case containing two reels and a length of magnetic tape that winds between them, used in audio or video tape recorders or players. What is a microcassette?

Chevette: A *small* model of a Chevrolet automobile

dinette: A *small* dining area in a house, usually with a built-in table and seats. Why would someone buy a **dinette set**?

Jeanette: A French girl's name meaning "*Little* Jean (John)." What other girls' names can you find that end in "-ette"? What conclusion can you draw from the names that you found?

leaflet: A *small* printed sheet, as for free distribution; a sheet of small pages folded but not stitched. The girls handed out leaflets describing their missing cat.

luncheonette: A *small* restaurant that serves only lunch, not dinners. The politician gave out **leaflets** at the luncheonette's door.

marionette: A small figure of a person operated from above with strings by a puppeteer

operetta (It., little opera): A musical-dramatic work with a *small* plot, cheerful music and spoken dialogue. Gilbert and Sullivan wrote many popular operettas, including *HMS Pinafore, Pirates of Penzance, and The Mikado.*

palette: French from Old French, small potter's shovel, diminutive of pale, shovel, spade

spinet: A *small*, compact upright piano or electronic organ. Since these instruments are not small spines, can you find the origin of this word?

toilet [French for small + toile (cloth)]: Act or process of bathing, hairdressing, use of cosmetics, and dressing. Only in the U.S. does it mean a bathroom.

What do the following mean?

brunette _____

kitchenette _____

omelette _____

owlet _____

ranchette _____

starlet: Not a *little* star in the sky, but a _____

statuette _____

booklet _____

cigarette _____

eaglet _____

Nicorette _____

What is the name of Winnie-the-Pooh's best friend? Do you believe the author, A.A. Milne, chose a good name for him? Why or why not? _____
_____

What brand of chewing gum uses this suffix in its name? What does its name mean? _____

How many Spanish words do you know that end in -ito/-ita, Spanish for "little"? Here are a few. Add yours below.

gallito: rooster

hermanito: Little brother

burrito: Little donkey (?)

perito: Little dog (puppy)

Bernardette: _____

bathinette/bassinette: _____

baguette: _____

brunette: _____

Your additions: _____

2. **Acronyms**, including intriguing gasoline brands (SUNOCO©, MOBIL©, TEXACO©, etc.), and HOV, TGIF©, HAZMAT and so on — words many of us say without knowing or even wondering about their meanings, but once we do, we remember them. In fact, this is quick learning; no need for reinforcement. Answers in Appendix, Page 219

3. **Automobile cognomens**: What do they mean? Do they fit the model? Why or why not? How do they apply to a car? What is a caprice? Can a Dodge be intrepid? Look for these when you're out and around and keep a list of others with interesting names. The advantage of this type of word is that invariably once students gain this sort of awareness, they will look for— and question— other models' names. Answers in Appendix, Page 219

    a. *Cabriolet*
    b. (Chevy) *Caprice*
    c. *Cavalier*
    d. *Envoy*
    e. (Dodge) *Intrepid*
    f. (Oldsmobile) *Intrigue*

g. *Legacy*

h. *Odyssey.*

4. **Sports team names** will intrigue children, especially when they learn their significance. Which ones interest them? Do their names relate to their locations? Why/why not? Explain. How did you form your answers? Can you add to the list? Answers in Appendix Pages 219-220

   a. Baltimore Orioles

   b. Dallas Mavericks

   c. Detroit Pistons

   d. Green Bay Packers

   e. New York Knickerbockers

   f. Orlando Magic

   g. Philadelphia 76ers

   h. Pittsburgh Steelers

   i. San Diego Padres

   j. Utah Jazz

5. **Product names**

   *"The more words you know, the more clearly and powerfully
   you will think and the more ideas you will invite into your mind."*
   Wilfred Funk

Just as with vehicles and teams, every product needs a name. Creators often draw upon basic root words from Latin or Greek, or they combine syllables of several words to invent a new name. Although the list of these is almost endless, I share a few I like. I'll hope you will be watching along with me for new ones that are sure to pop up!

Think about this: To how many products' names do we ever give thought? How important are these to the marketing and acceptability of the product? (Think "Obsession" for a perfume.) Does they draw buyers? Decisions governing the naming of a product must take almost as much time and thought as the development of the product itself!

Newspaper flyers at drugstores and grocery stores, along with ads in newspapers and magazines, will get you started on them. You will also need to "Google" some of the names in order to fully understand them. **WARNING**: Once you begin thinking about these, other products' names may tickle your brain.

Those listed below followed by an* indicate a connection to a Latin or Greek root, prefix, or suffix. A good mind game is to ponder the reasons manufacturers choose the names they do. Why Arrid˚? Cascade˚? Efferdent˚? Unisom˚? Lubriderm˚? Vitalis˚? Understanding these products' names produces astute students.

Alluna˚:Sleep by the <u>moon</u> *
Astroturf˚ *_____
Benefiber˚ *_____
Caterair˚ Catering to airplanes
Clorox˚
Comet˚ *_____
Cetaphil˚ Lover of oil *
Comsat˚ Communication satellite
Dyna<u>vite</u>˚ Dynamic + <u>vita</u>min *
Flexamatic˚ Automatically flexible
Frigidaire˚ Cold air
Habitrol˚ Habit control (to control cigarette smoking)
Hydrience˚ Water + condition *
Kudos˚ (granola bar): Credit for an achievement; glory
Magnavox˚: Large voice (the product that started me on all this!) *
Maxipedic˚: Large + orthopedic (mattress) *
Nicoderm˚: Nicotine + skin (a skin patch to control cigarette   smoking) *
Nicorette˚ (gum): Small nicotine *
Ore-Ida˚: Oregon + Idaho (potatoes)
Oust˚ *_____
Polyvisol˚: Many + vitamins + soluble *
Pyrex˚: Able to withstand <u>???</u> *
Renuzit˚: Renews it
Rhinocort˚:
Teleflora˚: Distant flowers *
Thermos˚: Temperature container for keeping food hot *
Thermador˚: (temperature / heat + ?): a stove *
Thermosilk˚_____
Visine˚: eye/see + medicine *
* Uses a Latin or Greek root

MORE VOCABULARY Page 238 in Appendix

Probe and Shed Light

CHAPTER IV

▼

A PRECEPT FOR
INTERDISCIPLINARY CURRICULA

"Whether individual differences in ability are innate or are due to environmental differences, we must deal with them imaginatively and constructively."
John Gardner

Once we were all settled into our Banner's daily routine, I could now do what I had been longing for when I had wished I had "a school of my own." Although I spent considerable time on publicity and discovered I had abilities to write successful grant proposals and school plays, my true function was to put my teaching and curriculum experience to work. In fact, I was doing what homeschoolers have been doing all along!

I wanted to imbue our students with cultural literacy by using literature beyond the basal reader, including exposure to Shakespeare and Chaucer; furnish them with a rich and pertinent vocabulary; provide for art history instruction; and introduce numerous forms of music, including grand opera.

I also wanted to establish techniques that presented instruction in ways that assured learning for all students. Providing for constant review in all areas was one of them, because, what students understand for the moment is soon forgotten. This was my philosophy when I required each week's new vocabulary words to be used frequently in classroom discussions and written work.

Prior to founding Banner, I had recognized that it is the rare child who enjoys and excels in all areas of schoolwork. In fact, many children may be very bright but still struggle through their school years because some type of learning disability or their own personal tastes inhibit their performance. Furthermore, many children do not fall conveniently into an age-grade constraint. A child's mental readiness, skills' mastery or intellect may be either above or below that considered normal for that grade/age. Homeschooling takes care of these.

While I was teaching before Banner, the more convinced I became that finding material which suits all students in the same grade is neither easy nor necessary. I also thought that when a topic had strong appeal for the students, the customary time was all too short, leaving me to choose what seemed logical by prolonging the study and introducing material from other sources or adhering to a schedule already laid out.

The former choice felt like teaching; the latter did not. The more I thought about this dilemma, the surer I became that students who are immersed in a special topic for an extended period will learn—and retain—far more than they would when using standard textbooks. This thinking was coupled with my objection to the irrelevant assemblies with a speaker or entertainer whose programs are unrelated to any subject in which students are currently (or were recently) engaged.

From my viewpoint, unless students have been prepared for visitors and are involved in follow-up discussions, these events are just entertainment and a waste of a school's time and money. Similarly, field trips taken just for fun prove unproductive. A visit to a zoo, for instance, when students haven't studied animals beforehand, will make far less impact than when students are prepared for what they will encounter.

These thoughts led me to search for a better way to provide students with the instruction in subject matter apart from the necessary drills and practice of specific skills. My goal was to find ways to excite and engage students in specific learning. Now, I was in a position to spread my ideas to a much greater audience!

My deliberations resulted in my deciding to choose science and social studies subjects that would stretch across all disciplines and be treated from a variety of perspectives for all grades. My expectations were that such a method would not only deepen students' knowledge but would also appeal to a wide range of learners.

It definitely did, as I will never forget the morning when I visited our middle school (at a different location then than our primary building) just as the students were arriving. They were actually pushing and shoving to get <u>into</u> the building so that they could show the principal the work they'd done the night before. "Look!" "Look what I did!" were the general cries.

Once you see a sight like this, you know you are reaching your students. Not only are they learning subject content, they are obviously enjoying school, something that certainly is not always the case. Using such an approach causes students to transform from disengaged learners to active participants.

Probe and Shed Light

One major advantage of units like these is the variety of materials and projects that students can employ. A walk around our classrooms would show children sitting side by side, one reading a pop-up book, the other a *National Geographic*. Primary school students are not aware of the differences between these materials; each learns in his own way and is able to share in discussions and projects. This method fits with what we recognize as success building success and increasing confidence.

Although these topics took a fair amount of preparation, especially for the first round, our teachers found the planning sessions stimulating. Each of us interjected our ideas and took responsibility for our areas of special interest.

Before the outset of Banner's second year, we chose mammals as our first interdisciplinary topic. During the summer, I gathered information from numerous local resources for field trips and speakers and outlined ideas for art, music, and phys. ed. I provided teachers with an annotated and relevant vocabulary. At our fall planning session, teachers, including those of art, music, and gym, contributed ideas to add to this theme.

We created our own study guide from the following:

a. *A Field guide to the Mammals* by William Burt
b. *Audubon Society's Field Guide to North American Mammals*
c. Material from text books, magazines, such as *Ranger Rick*, relevant newspaper articles, Fish and Wildlife tracts, etc.
d. Local newspapers apprised us of area experts, museums, art galleries, and the like.
e. Public schools' resource centers, public libraries and their librarians, and parents knowledgeable about specific topics.

We limited our study, with a few exceptions, to North American mammals, beginning with the most primitive, in this case marsupials ('possums), and progressing over three months to the most advanced, the primates.

Our students' interest never waned, and I feel certain that others who wish to do a similar study will encounter the same result. Children brought their own pets to school when they fit the current order; a wolf visited along with his owner; and we spent several hours at a nearby zoo with study sheets in hand. A local veterinarian added other dimensions. First and second graders, so eager to read various materials, made quantum leaps with their reading skills.

The following description of our mammal study is a model for any topic and works especially well when all students, regardless of grade, are involved in examining the same topic. Perhaps the best reason for using these types of topics is because they are likely to involve reluctant learners, as there is something for all students in keeping with their interests and abilities.

In following years, we applied the same techniques we had used with mammals, to other topics: Fish; insects; water; inventions and inventors; human body; reptiles and amphibians; geology; birds; winds and weather; the solar system. Vocabularies are below.

I hope that homeschoolers in the same general area will choose simultaneous topics and perhaps produce a play or other cooperative efforts for the benefit of everyone attending the same conference, a gathering where experts in the field of their joint studies could provide more information. Or, homeschooling groups might consider setting up an annual succession of topics, so that materials from one group could be used the next year by another, thus saving money for materials.

A. Mammals: Our First Immersion (for which we received an Exemplary Award from the State of Maryland)

A study of dinosaurs, a topic of high interest for most children, preceded the mammal study. We studied mammal orders as they progress from those scientists consider the most primitive to the most advanced, focusing on those found mostly in North America, although we did include some animals of special interest to children from other continents.

Science labs were where much excitement took place. On hand, we had a collection of skulls and preserved animals gathered from veterinarians, museums, wildlife organizations, and college collections. In addition to providing "hands-on" experiences for the students, the labs strengthened students' observational powers and provided them with opportunities for problem solving. A succession of students' pets allowed everyone to study the characteristics of different orders of mammals. We were fortunate that a nearby zoo manager brought small animals for students to observe.

The supporting vocabulary (shown below) enhanced the entire course of study. Words such as carnivore, nocturnal, hibernate, digitigrade, terrestrial, and aquatic are concepts in themselves, but we broke them into their components and recombined with other roots, prefixes, and suffixes to give students a more complete understanding (examples: carnivore: carnival; nocturnal, nocturne, etc.). We enriched students' language further by using expressions such as "pussyfooting," "harebrained," "shrewish," and "dog-eared."

We planned this study to include all disciplines, which meant social studies classes covered animal range maps and topics of ecology and habitat, while animals in folk tales and mythological beasts pranced across the pages of literature. We measured the comparative heights and weights of our resident or visiting animals and their (and our students') length of jumps and hops.

Art classes turned skulls, feet, body structure, and proportion into interesting lessons. In music, the *Carnival of Animals*, *Waltzing Matilda*, and *Old MacDonald*, among others, added a lilting note to the study. Gym classes for the younger students incorporated kangaroo hops, bear steps, etc.

Field trips were integral to our study. A visit to the zoo allowed students to see both types of animal feet and introduced them to assorted endangered species. A video of *Never Cry Wolf* made an enjoyable culminating experience, especially when students called out many of "their" vocabulary words.

Older students learned about the uses of animals to man and became aware of the problems connected with the conservation of species. We discussed the environmental issues of habitat loss, the role of predators as viewed by different elements in today's society, the use of pesticides, and human versus animal needs.

Guest speakers increased students' awareness of careers in veterinary medicine, pathology, animal husbandry, zoology, and zoo management. We were fortunate to have domestic breeds, such as goats, sheep, and llamas, as visitors.

This study required a wealth of books, magazines, pamphlets, posters, study prints, games, and videos, many of which were available through our local Media Center.

Now that computers are regular components of homes and schools, I suggest adding an important facet to this type of multi-disciplined topics, that of building databases of information on the subject. Older students should learn how to add and retrieve information, as well as how to maintain an annotated bibliography of books and articles that were used. Computers can also provide a networking environment in which students may collect and analyze information, then share sources of materials and discoveries with other homeschoolers.

With the success of our first immersion, we continued to plan similar science topics for the start of each school year. The vocabularies below reflect our specific studies.

B. Science Immersions and Vocabulary
(I note spelling challenges with an * and those that are also concepts with a C)

1. **Birds**
   beak & bill: Synonyms for the horny projection forming a bird's jaws

camouflage (v): To disguise something. Female birds' feathers help camouflage them when they are on the nest. C *

eyrie (or aerie): An eagle's or crow's nest; a lookout   C   *

female (n): The mother bird   C

male (n): The father bird   C

mandibles: The upper and lower parts of the bill

molt (v): To drop old feathers so that new ones can grow in   C

preen (v): To trim and clean feathers with the beak. Sometimes people preen in from of mirror.   C

primary feathers (n): The large stiff feathers on the end joint of a bird's wing

stoop (n & v): A steep dive made by birds of prey

talon (n): A bird's claw. Eagles, hawks, and owls have large talons.

2. **Geology**

alloy: A mixture of two or more metals   C

basalt: A hard, dense, dark volcanic rock, often having a glassy appearance

bituminous (adj); Able to burn, such as bituminous coal*

conglomerate (adj): Made up of separate parts or substances collected together into a single mass; in geology, made up of rock fragments or pebbles cemented together in a mass of hardened clay and sand. Explain: English is a conglomerate language. **conglomeration** (n): Consisting of things collected from various sources. She had a conglomeration of souvenirs in her drawer. **C**

fissure: A cleft or crack. The leaf was caught in the fissure.

gem: A precious or, occasionally, a semiprecious stone, cut and polished for use as a jewel

geo-: Earth: geology, geography, geothermal, geode   C

igneous (adj): Rock formed from the solidification of molten rock material

lith: Stone: megalith, monolith, lithograph   C

mega-: Large: megalith, megaton   C

metamorphic: A rock changed in structure or composition by heat, pressure, or chemical process, usually while buried deep below Earth's surface.

-ology: Study of, or science of: geology, biology, zoology   **C**

petr-: Stone, rock: petrify, petroleum, petroglyph, petrology   C

sediment: Matter or mass deposited by water or wind; **sedimentary** rocks are in layers formed by the accumulation of matter that settles on a bottom or collects on a surface.

3. Human Body

animate (adj/v): Living, having life; (v): to give life to. She was quite animated when she won the prize. **inanimate** (adj) not alive. Rocks are inanimate. C

appendix (n): A small saclike appendage of the large intestine; also, additional material at the end of a book

artificial (adj): Opposite of natural; not real: artificial respiration; artificial leg / arm; artificial flowers   * C

aud-: Root word meaning "hear": audible, audience, auditorium; inaudible C

blind (adj): (1) Not able to see, unseeing. She was blind to all the beauty around her. (2) A hiding place from which to watch or hunt wildlife.

cardio-: Root word meaning heart: cardiac, cardiology, cardiogram, endocarditis C

charlatan (n): A person who pretends to have knowledge or ability that he does not have. That doctor is a charlatan.   *

chronic (adj): Continuing for a long time. She has a chronic illness. He is a chronic complainer.   C

derm-: Skin: dermatitis, dermatologist, endoderm C

digest (v): To change food in the body so it can be absorbed; to think over, absorb mentally; to condense or summarize information

digit (n): Finger or toe. I have 20 digits.

dumb (adj): Speechless. People who are deaf are often also unable to speak, hence the old-fashioned phrase no longer in use, "deaf and dumb." I was struck dumb by the news. Our pets are dumb animals. C

elbow grease (n): Lots of effort; physical effort used to do a job. I used a lot of elbow grease to get the floor clean. C

encephela-: The brain: encephalitis, electroencephalogram (EEG)

fatal (adj): Deadly. He had a fatal accident / disease / illness / wound. I made a fatal mistake. He made a fatal move in chess / checkers. fatality (n): death C

handicap (n): Any disadvantage that makes success more difficult. Being *blind* is often a handicap. The best golfer was given the highest handicap. * C

hemo- : Blood; hemoglobin, hemostat, hemophiliac, hemorrhage C

hygiene (n): The science of health and its maintenance; system of principles for the preservation of health and prevention of disease. We should all practice good hygiene. * C

hypochondria (n): Abnormal anxiety about one's health, often an imaginary illness. From the Greeks, who thought the problem arose when the spleen that lay under (hypo) the cartilage of the breastbone (chondros). hypochondriac (n): A person with this anxiety *

-itis (suffix meaning inflammation.) Appendicitis is the inflammation of the appendix; tonsillitis; arthritis: joint + itis. C

lean (adj): Without fat. I eat lean meat. Lean, mean Joe Green! We live in lean times. She has a lean look. C

Probe and Shed Light

mortal (n): That which eventually must die; deadly, fatal; **immortal**: not mortal, deathless, living forever. He received a mortal wound. They are mortal enemies. mortality, immortality C

mute (adj): Not able to speak; silent; a device on a musical instrument to soften its tone. A mute swan does not have a call. Some deaf people are mute. C

obese (adj): Very fat (from Latin "that has eaten itself"). He is obese. obesity (n): fatness

-ology: The study of: biology, geology; **-ologist** one who studies: dermatologist, cardiologist C

ortho-: Straight, upright: orthopedic, orthopod, orthodox C

panacea (n): Cure-all. Some people regard aspirin as a panacea. *

pneuma- / pneumo: Air, wind; lung: pneumonia, pneumatic drill C

spire: To breathe: respire, inspire, expire, conspire, aspire, transpire. Spirit is related. C

torso (n): The body of a person (or animal) except for the head and limbs

vis-: Root word meaning see: invisible, vision, visit, visitor, vista, vis à vis (face to face) C

vita-: Life: vitamin [vita + min (amino)]; vital: concerned with life; important: vital organs, vital message, vital statistics; vitality; revitalize; Vitalis® (hair conditioner) C

4. **Insects**

abdomen: The belly of an insect *

ambush (v): To hide for a surprise attack. The spider ambushed the fly.

antennae (n): The sensory appendages on the head of an insect; a feeler. Compare these to those used in the past to connect to television. C *

apiary (n): A place where bees are kept. **apiarist** (n) A person who keeps bees *

arthropods (jointed feet): Insects, spiders, centipedes, shrimp, and crab

boll weevil: A small, long-snouted beetle of Mexico and the southern United States that punctures cotton buds and whose larvae hatch and damage cotton bolls, the seed-bearing capsule of cotton *

bumble (v): To move clumsily, as a bumble bee appears to do. He bumbled into the chair.   C

camouflage (n): Concealment by disguise or protective coloring * C

cocoon (n): A protective case of silk or similar material spun by the larvae of moths and other insects that serves as a natural protective covering, such as the egg case of a spider

cryptic (adj): Hidden, secret. Animals with cryptic coloring are camouflaged. Walking sticks (insects) are cryptic. Her expression was cryptic. * C

diurnal (adj): Active in the daytime. Bees are diurnal. C

entomology (n): The branch of zoology that deals with insects; **entomologist**

industrious (adj): Hard working. Ants are industrious.

insecticide: (insect + kill) (n): A product that kills different types of insects *

iso-: Same: isoptera (same wing size). Butterflies belong to the isoptera order of insects.   C

larva (n): The newly hatched, wingless, often wormlike form of many insects before metamorphosis; **larvae**: plural

metamorphosis (n): A marked change in the <u>form</u> of an animal, as when the larva of an insect changes to a pupa or a tadpole becomes a frog * **C**

nocturnal (adj): Active at night. I enjoy the crickets' nocturnal chorus. Most owls are nocturnal.

ortho-: Straight, upright: orthoptera (straight wing) C

parasite (n): A plant or animal that lives with another and at whose expense it gets its food, shelter, etc. Fleas are a dog's parasites. C

petiole (n): A slender, stalk-like part, as that connecting the thorax and abdomen in certain insects

predator (n): An animal that devours another. Birds are insects' predators, and a praying mantis is a moth's predator.   C

prey (n): An animal hunted or killed for food by another animal. The mosquito was the spider's prey. (v) to hunt or kill other animals for food. C

-pter (suffix meaning feather or wing): Orthoptera (straight wing), Lepidoptera (scaly wing): butterflies C

thorax (n): The second or middle region of the body of an arthropod, between the head and the abdomen, in most insects

Extra words for spelling challenges: Caterpillar, centipede, cicada, exoskeleton, katydid, mosquitoes, spiracles

5. Machines and Inventions

benchmark: A surveyor's mark made on a permanent landmark that has a known position and altitude. Benchmarks are used as reference points in determining other altitudes or measurements. C

circa: Latin for "around/more or less." The first machine of this kind was invented circa 1895.

copyright: Protection from copying of literary, dramatic, musical, and artistic works. Copyrights are registered in the Copyright Office of the Library of Congress.

inert: Without power to move; inactive

innovation: Something newly introduced; new method, device, etc.; a change in the way of doing things. **innovator**: One who creates C

milestone: A stone or pillar set up to show the distance in miles to or from a specified place; a significant or important event in the career of a person or in the history of anything C

Probe and Shed Light

obsolete: No longer in use or practice. Hand-cranked telephones are obsolete. Computers may make letter writing obsolete. C

patent: A grant issued by the U. S. Government giving an inventor the right to exclude all others from making, using, or selling his invention within the U. S., its territories and possessions

Rube Goldberg: Super-complicated inventions to do super-simple things, named for a cartoonist who drew ridiculous contraptions

rudimentary: Elementary, basic. The neophyte inventor had only rudimentary knowledge of the lever.

simulate: To pretend to be something that is not. There were simulated flowers on the simulated wood table. C

trademark: A brand name or logo, as a word, symbol, design or combination of these used by a merchant or manufacturer to identify its goods or services and distinguish them from those manufactured or sold by others

6. Mammals

albino (n): A person, animal or plant lacking in pigment and is, therefore, unnaturally white. Albinos have the quality of **albinism.** (adj): He rode an albino horse. Antonym is **melanism,** having excessive dark pigments. C

aquatic (adj): Growing or living in water. Seals are aquatic. C *

arboreal (adj): Inhabiting or frequenting trees. Many primates are arboreal. C

browse (v): To feed on or nibble at leaves or twigs; to graze in a field. How can you browse through a book? A store? The Internet? C

carnivore (n): Meat eating. **carnivorous** (adj). Lions are carnivorous animals because they are carnivores. * **C**

carrion (n): The decaying flesh of a dead body. Some mammals, birds, and insects feed on carrion. *

-dactyl (n): Finger, toe, digit: pterodactyl (wing + digit)

denizen (n): An inhabitant of a place. Mice are denizens of fields. The denizens of that apartment building are noisy. * **C**

dent-/dont-: Tooth or teeth: rodent, dental, dentist, denture, dentifrice, dentate, orthodontist, periodontist, indent, dandelion (tooth of the lion), **edentate** (adj): Without teeth. Anteaters, armadillos, and sloths are edentates. C

derm-: Skin, pachyderm (thick + skin) an elephant C

digit (n): Finger or toe

digitigrade (adj): Type of foot in which only the digits bear on the ground; walking on the digits. Most mammals and all birds are digitigrade. (See plantigrade below.) * **C**

diurnal (adj): Active in daytime. Most mammals are diurnal. **C**

domesticate (v): To tame animals or plants that are no longer wild. They have been **domesticated**. They are domestic animals. **C**

estivate (v): Remain dormant during the summer (opposite of *hibernate*); also, to remain inactive during the heat of the day. Many desert animals estivate. **C**

fecund (adj): Fertile, fruitful, productive, prolific. Rabbits and mice are especially fecund. C

feral (adj): Untamed, undomesticated — hence, wild. C

hare: Similar to a rabbit but having longer ears and legs and giving birth to active, furred young

herbivore (n): Plant eater. Sheep are herbivores. Cats are not.

hibernate (v): To winter; to pass the winter in an inactive state. Bears hibernate; squirrels sometimes hibernate. * **C**

hirsute (adj): Hairy, shaggy, bristly. Apes are hirsute.

lagomorph (hare + shape) (n): Plant-eating mammals, such as rabbits, hares and pikas

mammal (n): Any of various warm-blooded vertebrate animals of the class *Mammalia*, including human beings, characterized by a covering of hair on the skin and, in the female, milk-producing mammary glands for nourishing the young C

masticate (v): To chew. Mammals masticate their food.

melanistic (adj): Dark coloration of the skin, hair, fur, or feathers because of a high concentration of melanin. Having unnatural dark pigment, as with some squirrels.

menagerie (n): A collection of wild or strange animals kept in cages or enclosures for exhibition

morph-: Root word meaning shape or form: lagomorph, shape of a hare

nocturnal (adj): Active at night. Most in the cat family are nocturnal. **C**

omnivore (n): Eating both vegetable and animal food. Goats are omnivores. **omnivorous** (adj) **C**

-ped, -pod, -pus: Foot: Biped (2-footed), quadruped; pedestrian, pedestal, anthropod, octopus **C**

plat- : Flat. Platypus, platform, plateau

plantigrade (adj): Type of foot wherein the heel touches the ground. Primates, bears, and 'possums are plantigrade animals. (See *digitigrade*.)

primate (n): The order of mammals—man, apes, monkeys, marmosets and lemurs—considered to be **first** in rank or importance **C**

proboscis (n): An elephant's trunk; a long, flexible snout; a large nose. Proboscis monkeys live In Borneo. *

quarry (n): Anything being hunted or pursued. The tiger followed his quarry. *

rhino-: Root word meaning "pertaining to the nose": rhinoceros, rhinitis, rhinology, rhinoplasty, rhinoscope **C**

ruminate (v): To chew again what has been chewed and swallowed as cows, goats, sheep, deer, and giraffes do; to bring to mind and consider again and again. He ruminated all day on the plan for the fair. **C**

scat (n): Animal droppings. There was scat next to the cat's spoor.

shrewish (adj): Having the qualities of a shrew; a scolding disposition

simian (adj): Apelike. The zoo displayed simian twins. (Don't get this confused with Siamese twins!)

skulk (v): To move or lurk about in a stealthy manner. The lion skulked in the tall grass.

slothful (adj): Sluggish, lazy; moving like a sloth, a slow-moving, arboreal, edentate mammal of South and Central America, having long hook-like claws by which they hang upside down from tree branches while feeding on leaves, buds, and fruits

sly (adj): Clever, cunning, crafty. Foxes are sly.

spoor (n): Animal tracks. We followed the platypus's spoor for several miles. **C**

terrestrial (adj): Belonging to the land; of the earth. Rabbits are terrestrial but sloths are not.

vigilant (adj): Watchful. Deer are vigilant when browsing. **C**

vixen (n): A female fox; a shrewish, ill-tempered woman. Shakespeare wrote "*The Taming of the Shrew*."

voracious (adj): Greedy in eating, ravenous; excessively eager; a voracious eater. Does a voracious reader eat books?   **C**

warren (n): A space or limited area in which rabbits breed or are numerous; any building or city street crowded like a rabbit warren

wary (adj): Cautious of danger, careful. The domestic cat was wary of the feral dog.

wily (adj): Crafty, sly. The wily wolf tracked the spoor of the rodent.

zoology (n): Study of animals (zoo + ology)

Some interesting idioms based on animal behavior:

badger (v): To pester. Please don't badger me!

(the) **cat's meow**: It's the best!

catty ("meow!") (adj): Saying mean things behind a person's back. She's really a catty person.

dog tired: Worn out

ferret (out): Find out information

harebrained (adj): Heedless, not very smart. The boy's plan was harebrained.

horse around: Fool around

hound's tooth: A woven pattern of material

lionize: Make larger than life. Many celebrities are lionized.

lion's share: More than others get

monkey around: Fool around

mousey: Plain-looking and quiet. Often people you think are mousey turn out to be a lot of fun.

outfox: Outsmart

play possum: Pretend to be asleep or dead

rat (v): Tattle

skunk (v): Cheat. I was skunked out of my vacation.

squirrel away: Save, hide. The miser squirreled away his savings.

weasel out of it: Wiggle one's way out of a promise or job

wolf it down

work like a beaver

Mammals spelling challenges: Elephant, rabbit, rhinoceros, squirrel

7. Reptiles and Amphibians

amphibious (adj): Able to live on both land and water [amphi (on both sides) + bios (life)], like frogs and salamanders. Some boats, airplanes, and vehicles are amphibious. * **C**

crocodile tears (n): False tears, not truly expressing any sadness. Crocodiles look as though they are shedding a tear or two, but they are not. Children frequently shed crocodile tears in the hopes of getting their own way. **C**

diurnal (adj): Active during the daytime rather than at night. Antonym of estivate. * **C**

estivate (v): To remain inactive during the heat of the day. Most reptiles estivate. Many creatures in deserts estivate.

reptilian (adj): Like a reptile; sneaky, mean

-saur(suffix): Lizard. saurian (adj): lizard-like; dinosaur

serpent: Snake. **serpentine** (adj): Coiled or twisted, winding, turning often, like the movement of serpents. A serpentine river flows near my house. **C**

venom (n): Poison introduced by some snakes, insects, etc., into the body of the victim; spite, malice. **venomous** (adj)

wary (adj): Cautious, careful, suspicious of. The frog was wary of the boy.*

8. Space and Astronomy

astronomical: Very large, as the numbers or quantities that belong to astronomy. She has an astronomical number of books. * **C**

celestial: Of the heavens or sky; heavenly. Stars are celestial objects.

gibbous moon: When the moon is in a phase between half-moon and full moon and the curves forming its outline are convex. A **waxing gibbous moon** appears to grow larger toward a full moon. A **waning gibbous moon** appears to grow smaller after a full moon.

helio-: The sun: heliograph, heliotrope (flower that opens only when it's sunny), heliotropism

luna-: Moon; lunar, lunatic, luna moth, *Au Clair de la Lune*

moonlight (v): To work a second job, usually at night

moonshine: Unlawfully-made whiskey, made at night "under the light of the moon"

once in a blue moon: A second full moon in the same month, which does not happen very often. Once in a blue I get to play chess with my grandfather. **C**

wax and wane: Grow larger, then smaller or lesser. The pain in her ankle waxed and waned. The sound of the siren waxed and waned. The moon waxes and wanes. **C**

9. **Water**

aqua: Water – aquamarine, aquatic, aquarium, aquaplane, Aquarius, aqueduct, aqueous   **C**

brine: Salt water; **briny**: of or like brine, very salty

cascade: (n) Waterfall; anything that ripples or showers down; (v) to flow down. We picnicked beside the roaring cascade. His books cascaded off the desk.   **C**

ebb and flow: Lowering and rising of a sea's tide or of a person's interest in a subject   **C**

fathom: A unit of measure equal to 6 feet, used mainly in measuring the depth of water

flotsam and jetsam: Flotsam is the wreckage of a ship or of its cargo found floating on the sea or washed up on the shore. Jetsam is anything thrown overboard from a ship.

hydr-: Water: hydrant, hydroplane, hydraulic, hydrogen, dehydrate, hydrophobia, hydroelectricity, hydrographer, hydrotherapy, hydrofoil, hydrothermal. Hydras grow in fresh water.   **C**

league: About 3 nautical miles *

marine: Of the sea or ocean; inhabiting, found in, or formed by the sea. We studied marine mammals. The **Marine Corps**, a branch of the United States armed forces, is equipped and trained for land, **sea**, and aerial combat but is most closely associated with the sea. **mariner**: A sailor or seaman **C**

naut: Ship or sailor: nautical, nautilus, astronaut, cosmonaut, Argonaut

potable: Drinkable, safe to drink. The water in most rivers is not potable.

tributary: A stream or river that flows into a larger one. The Mississippi River has many tributaries.

10. Weather and Winds

abate: To lessen. The force of the wind abated.

anemo-: Wind: An anemom´eter measures wind. Anemones (pronounced anem´oneese) are wind flowers. **C**

austral (adj): Southern. The austral winds warmed us.   **C**

boreal (adj): Northern. The boreal winds made us shiver. Boreal Owls live in the boreal forest. **C**

barometer (n): An instrument for measuring atmospheric pressure, used especially in weather forecasting

cirrus cloud (n): A high-altitude cloud composed of narrow bands or patches of thin, generally white, fleecy parts *

cumulus cloud (n): A dense, white, fluffy, flat-based cloud with a multiple rounded top and a well-defined outline. Accumulate is related.

doldrums (n): A part of the ocean near the equator where there are strange calms and baffling winds; a state of listlessness or boredom **C**

drought (n): Lack of rain or moisture. Corn does not grow well when there is a drought. *

inclement (adj): Harsh, severe, unkind. The weather was as inclement as the old man next door. **C**

inundate (v): To flood. The river inundated the town. We were inundated with mail about the election. **C**

iso-: Same. Isotherms are lines on maps that connect the same temperatures.

leeward (usually pronounced loo´ard): On the protected side away from the wind; toward the wind. We sought shelter on the leeward side of the building. "They were sailing leeward." (See windward below.)

lightning (n): An abrupt, natural electric discharge in the atmosphere; (adj) Moving or occurring with remarkable speed or suddenness. She washed the dishes with lightning speed. *

meteorology (n): The science of weather. **meteorologist** *

monsoon: A seasonal wind of the Indian Ocean and southern Asia, blowing from the southwest from April to October, when it brings heavy rains, and from the northeast during the rest of the year

precipitation (n): Any form of water, such as rain, snow, sleet, or hail that falls to the earth's surface. *

prognosticate: To predict. Weathermen prognosticate the weather. *

rime: Frost. There was rime on the windows today.

temperature: (n): The degree of hotness or coldness of a body, an environment, water   *

tempest: A violent and extensive wind, especially one accompanied by rain, hail, or snow; any violent commotion. A small argument is said to be "A tempest in a teapot." **C**

thermo-: Heat: thermos bottle, thermometer, thermostat **C**

ventilate: To circulate fresh air. We ventilated the room. **ventilator, ventilation**

windward: The direction from which the wind blows. (opposite of leeward) **C**

zephyr: A gentle breeze, from Zephyrus, the Greek god of the west wind*

Names of winds: Chinook, maria (with a long i), mistral, roaring 40's, Santa Ana, trade winds. Winds may occur in the form of a cyclone, hurricane, tornado, twister, typhoon

11. Science References (in no specific order):

http://wwws.aimsedu.org/aims_store/Fall-Into-Math-Science-p-855.html
http://science.nasa.gov/
Open Directory - Kids and T
spaceweather.com.webloc
http://www.kidwings.com/owlpellets/
http://www.owlpages.com/articles.php?section=Owl+Physiology&title=Digestion
http://www.iit.cdu/~smile/bi8913.html
http://www.pelletsinc.com/

C. INTERDISCIPLINARY SOCIAL STUDIES TOPICS

> *"Send your students away from your instruction anxious to use what they have been taught—and eager to learn more."*
> **Robert Mager**. *Developing Attitude Toward Learning*

After our success with the mammal study, we were as keen as were the students to find similar pursuits. The more experience we gained with each unit, the easier the next became, even to the point of preparing students for snow days by assigning work on their projects.

Engaging students (and teachers) in one science and one major history topic each year brought excitement—along with a wealth of learning—to the everyday school routine.

The following general principles apply to any topic, although instructors, when designing and planning for implementation, must tailor specifics according to local resources and the interests and capabilities of those who will be involved in the activity.

Regional resources are your local newspapers, museums, art galleries, and area experts, including your relatives and friends. Keep a file on these. Research the holdings of your public library and consult its librarians. Subscribe to your area's public broadcast station so that you can use its program guide to prepare for upcoming television programs about your topic and to arrange to tape or rent them.

In many ways our immersion topics achieved the same results of those who promote learning communities or communities of practice. (See Etienne Wenger, *Communities of Practice*, as Published in the "*Systems Thinker*," June 1998.) Decades of research show that the more engaged students are, the more likely they are to learn (Nov. 5, 2007, *USA Today*).

William Whipple, in a speech presented at University of Miami, Jan. 9, 1998, "...conceives of knowledge not as something that is transferred in an authoritarian structure from teacher to student but rather as something that teachers and students work interdependently to develop. Thus it fosters active learning over passive learning, cooperation over competition, and community over isolation." I was quite pleased when I read the report in *USA Today* that validated this practice.

We selected a range of materials that students could process at their own level. The result was all students performed to their capacity with little chance of failure or frustration. The immersion method—that is, staying with one topic for a considerable amount of time—also ensures long-term learning for all students.

Social Studies: Immersions, Topics, and Vocabularies

Although the study of our own country's history, geography, government, holidays, languages, multiculturalism, religion, and current events is necessary for children's well-rounded education, our students showed little interest in these textbook/workbook topics. They fulfilled the necessary reading and assignments with little effort, although there was no air of excitement—and possibly little retention. We seldom witnessed any enthusiasm, even though we took field trips to relevant sites and brought appropriate speakers to Banner.

Therefore, with the insight we'd gained from our mammal study, we decided to plan a school-wide topic for up to four weeks each spring of our own and other countries' cultures. Our first one concentrated on various time periods in America's past; next came the Vikings. These topics were so overwhelmingly well received and students' interest so high that at the end of the four weeks that we had allotted for this topic, there was an outcry of "More! More!"

We continued to explore our own and other countries' way of life, including ancient and historical periods. Topics being almost endless, we had a broad array from which to choose, each of which easily met the requirements of students with varying abilities and learning styles.

Those we enjoyed at The Banner School while I was Head were: America's colonial period, Revolutionary War era, western movement, Native Americans; Vikings; Medieval life; Ancient Egypt; Ancient Greece and Rome; Mayas, Incas and Aztecs; modern-day Holland, Ireland, Japan, Africa, and India. It was also easy to compare and contrast our way of living with other countries and periods in the past.

Usually we immersed ourselves in an ancient culture, but the year the Olympics were held in Korea, we studied Korea and Japan. Any cultural or historic topic provides ample opportunities for reading and writing, critical thinking, vocabulary growth, as well as art and music enrichment. Field trips are easy to plan, speakers and materials abundant. We decided that as far as social studies topics went, it didn't matter what we chose, as choices were seemingly endless and all would bring cross-curricular results and lasting knowledge.

Many companies' catalogs offer high quality single-topic books. *(See a bibliography of these below.)* We used music, art, and gym classes to extend each topic, as did speakers, field trips, relevant terminology, banquets, and plays created especially for the subject. We found it a good idea to notify parents of our upcoming topic(s), since they may have articles to lend the class, or, if they wished, they could plan applicable family activities.

Deep involvement in our topics energized students as much as had the science ones, as students engaged in a variety of projects that differed greatly from their regular classroom work. We planned a four-to-five-year rotation for each major topic, because what children study in the early primary grades seems quite different to them four or five years later.

We had planned to repeat each of these subjects every five years, reasoning that those in the early primary grades would be different learners five years later. However, the second time we began the mammal study, we were in for a surprise! There was a cry of, "But we just did this!" A quick check revealed that, indeed, retention was very high, so we quickly added new ideas and materials to the study.

Despite the amount of advance preparation these topics took, we found the planning sessions stimulating. We each were able to interject our own ideas and to take responsibility for areas of special interest. (Among other tasks, I always chose vocabulary, spelling, and recitation challenges.) Everyone's two most favorite activities, aside from field trips, were the plays that incorporated additional factual material into its script and the culminating banquet befitting the culture and often served by parents.

Important Concepts:

a. The **Old World** consists of those parts of Earth known to Europeans, Asians, and Africans **before** the voyages of Christopher Columbus

b. The **New World** is one of the names used for the Americas. When the term originated in the late 15th century, the Americas were new to the Europeans, who previously thought the world consisted only of Europe, Asia, and Africa. The term "New World" should not be confused with "modern world," the latter generally refering to a historical period, not a landmass.

c. **pre-Columbian**: Period before Christopher Columbus discovered the New World

Integrating Vocabulary By Topics

A. General Ancient Cultures

alloy (n): A metal that is a mixture of two or more metals. Bronze is an alloy of tin and copper.

agrarian (adj): Pertaining to the land, farming. The Mayas were an agrarian people.

archeology (n): The scientific study of the life and culture of ancient peoples, as by excavating ancient cities. **archeologist** (n): One who undertakes such a study

artifact: (n): A simple object, such as a tool or ornament, showing human workmanship. Archeologists use artifacts to help them date a site.

authentic (adj): Real, genuine. The museum confirmed that the artifact was an authentic ancient shard. **authenticate** (v): The museum authenticated the archeologist's find.

barter (v): To trade for goods or services. The Native Americans bartered food from the White Men in exchange for beads.

cache (n): Hiding place. (v): To hide or store in a cache. We found many interesting artifacts cached in a cache.

circa (adj): When dating something to mean "around" or "about." This artifact was made circa 200 B.C.

glyph (noun): A carved figure, pictograph or hieroglyphic

heathen (n): A person regarded as uncivilized; a pagan *(q.v.)*

hieroglyphics (n): Picture writing; holy or secret carving. Being able to read hieroglyphics helps us to understand prehistoric cultures.

indigenous (adj): Native to. When Columbus and his men landed in the New World, they met the indigenous people. Maize was indigenous to the New World.

metallurgy (n): The art or science of separating metals from their ores and preparing them for use. Stone Age people had not learned metallurgy.

midden (n): A heap of bones, shells, etc., marking the site of a prehistoric dwelling. Archeologists seek kitchen middens.

nomad (n): Any person who has no permanent home and moves about constantly in search of food; a wanderer. Stone Age people were nomads. **nomadic** (adj): Some tribes of people are nomadic, as are caribou and other animals. Why are agrarian societies not nomadic?

pagan (n): One who has little or no religion or believes that death and oblivion are the natural end of life; one who delights in seeking after pleasure and material goods

paleo-: Prefix meaning ancient or prehistoric, as in Paleozoic, paleolithic, paleontologist

pre-Columbian (adj): Before Columbus's discovery of the New World. The museum had an exhibit of pre-Columbian pottery.

prehistoric (adj): Of the period before recorded history. The Celts lived in prehistoric times.

relic (n): An object, custom, etc., that has survived, wholly or partially, from the past

remnant (n): A small remaining part, a fragment left over, a trace. Today there are only remnants of Native American customs in the United States.

Probe and Shed Light

rudimentary (adj): Very basic, simple. The Aztecs had much more than rudimentary knowledge of astronomy.

Mathematical Contributions of the Mayas, Aztecs & Incas: A Native American Curriculum Unit for Middle & High School

shard (n): A fragment or broken piece, especially of pottery. All the artifacts were shards.

site (n): The place where something is, is to be, or was located. Archeologists look for the sites of ancient cities.

taboo (n): Forbidden, prohibited. In some ancient cultures, it was taboo for men and women to dance together. Some societies have many taboos. (Also spelled tabu)

B. Ancient Egypt

1. Interdisciplinary Guide to Ancient Egypt including notes on the opera Aida*

This 10-page illustrated guide includes details for advance planning and preparations; bibliography of literature; suggestions for writing, art, music, geography, math, science, and physical education; topics to research; suggestions for speakers, field trips, audio-visual aids and relevant activities; study materials and games; spelling challenges; comprehensive bibliography of resources; a sample letter to parents explaining the upcoming study, PLUS a guide for classroom viewing of the opera Aida, a gripping story for middle and high-schoolers.
*Available at www.seepub.com

2. Vocabulary

alabaster (n & adj): A translucent, whitish variety of gypsum used for vases, statues, etc., from the name of an ancient Egyptian town. "Thine alabaster cities gleam ..."

amulet (n): Something worn, often around the neck, as a protection against injury or evil; a charm

cartouche (n): A scroll-like ornament or tablet on Egyptian monuments; an oval figure containing the name of a ruler or deity **C**

delta (of Nile)(n): A deposit of sand and soil at the mouth of a large river, triangular in shape like the 4ᵗʰ letter of the Greek alphabet, delta (Δ)

dynasty (n): A succession of rulers who are members of the same family; the period during which a certain family reigns

Egyptian (n): A native or inhabitant of Egypt. (adj) relating to Egypt, its people or culture

hieroglyphics (n): Pictures or symbols representing words, syllables, or sounds used by the Egyptians and others instead of alphabetic letters

ibis (n): Any of several large wading birds with long legs, a long, slender neck, and a long bill. The Egyptians considered the ibis of the Nile to be sacred.

inundate (v): To cover with or as with a flood; deluge; flood. The Nile inundated the Egyptian village. The actor was inundated with fan mail. **C**

mummy (n): A dead body preserved by embalming

obelisk (n): A tall, four-sided stone pillar, tapering toward its pyramidal top. It often has hieroglyphics on it.

papyrus (n): A writing material created from a variety of tall water plants of the sedge family, formerly abundant in the Nile region of Egypt, and made by soaking, pressing, and drying thin slices of its pith laid crosswise. Our word paper comes from papyrus. *

pharaoh (n): The title of the rulers of ancient Egypt

pyramid (n): A huge structure with a square base and four triangular sides meeting at a point, each built by the Egyptians as royal tombs

sarcophagus (n): A limestone coffin or tomb, often inscribed and elaborately ornamented

scarab (n): A beetle, especially the black, winged dung beetle, held sacred by the Egyptians; an image of this beetle, cut from a stone or gem, often engraved with symbols on the flat underside, and formerly worn as a charm

scribe (n): A clerk, public writer or secretary. Many Egyptians used scribes to write letters for them.

Probe and Shed Light

sphinx (n): Any Egyptian statue or figure having the body of a lion and the head of a man, ram, or hawk. The best-known statue of this kind is at Giza, near Cairo, Egypt.

tomb (n): A burial place or receptacle for human remains

C. Ancient Greece and Rome

1. Literature: Aesop's Fables

2. Music: Orpheo & Eurydice, opera

3. Architecture: columns, pediments, Greek revival style of buildings

4. Greek alphabet: Alpha and Omega: The beginning and the end, similar from A to Z.

5. Use Roman numerals in a variety of exercises (see math topics below)

6. Challenge: Recite and write Greek Alphabet

7. http://en.wikipedia.org/wiki/Ancient_Roman_weights_and_measures

8. **Interdisciplinary Guide to Ancient Greece and Rome:** * A 12-page illustrated guide that includes the major and lesser gods of mythology; strange creatures; mythological places; words from the myths: our Greek and Roman heritage; five pages of graphics; suggested literature / texts for grades K-4 and 5-8; resources for art, music, math, audio-video, speakers, field trips, vocabulary (including relevant architecture terms); flower and plant names from Greek myths; product names based on Greek names and symbols; list of relevant poems; projects; spelling challenges; example of a chronogram; teacher guide.
    *Available at www.seepub.com

9. **Vocabulary**

    Achilles heel (from a Greek myth) (n): A vulnerable place on a person, even his feelings. She knew how to hurt him in his Achilles heel. **C**

alpha and omega (n): The first and last letters of the Greek alphabet, hence the beginning and ending of anything; similar to "from A to Z" **C**

amorous (adj): Loving, from the Greek god **Amor**. He is an amorous person.

boreal (adj): Northern, from the Greek god of the north wind, **Boreas**. Boreal owls live in cool and damp boreal forests. **C**

chaos (n): State of confusion, said to come from the state of the world before the Greek gods began to rule. The room was in chaos. **Chaotic** (adj): I had a chaotic afternoon. * **C**

cupidity (n): Love of material things, from the Roman god **Cupid**; greed

fauna and flora (n): Animal and plant life from Roman mythology. We studied the flora and fauna of the area. **C**

hygiene (n): The science of health and its maintenance, from the Greek goddess of health, **Hygea** * **C**

jovial (adj): Joyful, jolly, merry, from the Roman god **Jove**. He is such a jovial person!

lethargy (n): A state of inaction, drowsiness; prolonged and unnatural sleep, from Lethe, the river of forgetfulness in Greek and Roman myths. Occasionally, there is a feeling of lethargy in our classroom. **Lethargic** (adj): John was so lethargic that I took him to the doctor.

martial (adj): Military, from the Roman god of war, **Mars**. We listened to the martial music. Jane took a class in martial arts (judo, karate, etc.) * **C**

mentor (n): A wise, loyal advisor, from **Mentor**, the friend who counseled Odysseus (Ulysses)

morph- : Shape or form, from the Greek god **Morpheus** who could change his shape whenever he wanted. He was also the god of sleep. From this root words comes: morphine; metamorphosis (a marked change in the form of an animal, as when the larva of an insect changes to a pupa or a tadpole becomes a frog); lagomorph (shape of a hare); amorphous (without shape); endo- / meso- / ectomorph (three shapes of human bodies).

nectar and ambrosia (n): The drink and food of the gods. Today we drink apricot nectar and dine on a salad called ambrosia. * **C**

odyssey (n): A long, wandering journey, from the 10-year trip **Odysseus** took returning to Ithaca after the end of the Trojan War. We took a six-week odyssey to California * **C**

panic (n): Sudden, extreme and groundless fear, such as the god **Pan** caused

siren (n): An enticing, dangerous woman, from one of the minor Greek gods, represented with the heads, busts, and arms of women, said to lure sailors over to them, causing them to crash on rocks. Sirenia is an order of aquatic herbivorous (plant eating) mammals, such as the manatee.

spartan (adj): A person with spartan traits, meaning like a person from the city of **Sparta** who was hardy, stoical, highly disciplined, and without much comfort or luxury. He leads a spartan life; he lives in a spartan room. **C**

stentorian (adj): Extremely loud. From the Greek herald **Stentor** who had a very loud voice. She spoke in a stentorian way.

tantalize (v): To tempt or tease, from the Roman character **Tantalus**, who was condemned to reach forever for fruit and water always just beyond his grasp * **C**

titanic (adj): Huge! From the **Titans** whom the Greeks first thought ruled the world   **C**

vulcanize (v): To harden steel or rubber by heating, from the Roman god of fire, **Vulcan**

zephyr (n): The west wind, a soft, gentle breeze, so named by the Greeks*

Additional challenges for spelling: Aphrodite, Atalanta, Hercules, Mercury, Minotaur, Odysseus, Orpheus, Poseidon, Ulysses

D. Medieval/Middle Ages*

Reenactment Societies: Check with your local universities, as many support reenactors.

Society for Creative Anachronism: The SCA is the world's largest organization of Renaissance and medieval reenactment companies, with information on associated groups or 'kingdom's' around the globe, rules and regulations, membership info and related resources. Located in Cincinnati and Milpitas, California

The Directorie: The Web's most comprehensive and reliable list of Renaissance and medieval battle reenactments, encampments, feasts, pageants, and living history displays throughout the year

Trades and Occupations: Which of these trades are still being used? How many of these surnames/last names can you find in your telephone book?

Important Components of This Study:

1. Literature: Aesop's Fables
2. Ring Around the Rosy
3. London Bridge is Falling Down
4. Challenges for reciting or writing:

Prologue To Tales Of Canterbury

1st grade, lines 1-2 or 1-3; 2nd grade, lines 1-4 or 1-6;
3rd grade lines 1-6 or 1-9; 4-8th grade, all. Give translation.

Whan that Aprille with his shoures sote
The droghte of Marche hath perced to the rote,
And bathed every veyne in swich licour,
Of which vertu engendred is the flour;
When Zephirus eek with his swete breeth
Inspired hath in every holt and heeth
The tendre croppes, and the yonge sonne
Hath in the Ram his halfe cours y-ronne,
And smale fowles maken melodye...

Probe and Shed Light

When April with his showers sweet
The draught of March has pierced to the root
And bathed every vine in such liquor
Of which virtue the flower is engendered;
When Zepherus also with his sweet breath
Has inspired in every hold and heath
The tender crops, and the young sun
Has in the Ram his half course run,
And small birds make melody...

Interdisciplinary Guide to Medieval / Middle Ages: This 10-page illustrated guide includes details for advance planning and preparations; bibliography of literature; suggestions for writing, art, music (including historic information on London Bridge is Falling Down and Ring-Around-the-Rosy), geography, math, science, and physical education; a little bit of Chaucer; suggestions for speakers, field trips, audio-visual aids, and meaningful activities; spelling challenges; comprehensive bibliography of resources; a sample letter to parents explaining the upcoming study.
Available at www.seepub.com.

Trades and occupations: Which of those names below are still in use? How many of these surnames/last/ can you find in your telephone book?

bailey: From the French bailiff, a sheriff's assistant

baxter: Originally bakester, wife of a baker

blacksmith: A man who works, repairs, and shapes iron with a forge, anvil, hammer, etc.; a man who shoes horses

bloomer: Medieval ironworkers hammered metal into bars which they called 'blooms," and the craftsman who did it was called a bloomer.

chandler: A maker or seller of candles; a retailer of supplies and groceries, as in a ship's chandler

collier: A coal miner

cooper: A barrel maker

cordwainer: A leather-worker who makes items of cordovan (sheepskin or horsehide); a shoemaker

Probe and Shed Light

cutler: A knifesmith

farrier: A man who shoes horses; a blacksmith

fletcher (n): A person who makes or feathers arrows

franklin (n): A landowner of free but not noble birth, ranking just below the gentry

joiner: A carpenter, especially one who finishes interior woodwork, as doors, molding, stairs, etc.

mason: One who builds with stone or brick

miller: One who owns or operates a mill

palmer: A pilgrim who has been to the Holy Land and brought back a palm, or a piece of one, to prove it

reeve: The English word for sheriff's assistant

smith: A metal worker: silversmith, goldsmith, tin- / whitesmith

sutler: One who follows an army to sell food, liquor, etc., to its soldiers

teamster: One who drives a team (now, often, a truck) for hauling loads

thatcher: A man who makes a roof of straw, rushes, palm leaves, etc.; **thaxter**: his wife

turner: A man who works with a wheel or lathe to shape wood

wain- / wheelwright: A person who makes wheels

webster: A wife of a weaver or webb

wright: One who makes or constructs, as in shipwright, boatwright, housewright

Vocabulary

apprentice (n): A learner or beginner, especially at a craft or trade **C**

banquet (n): A big meal elaborately prepared or served *

Probe and Shed Light

barbarian (n): A member of a people or group with a civilization regarded as primitive, savage

calligraphy (n): Ornamental handwriting; **calligrapher**

castle (n): A fortified stronghold, now converted to residential use **C**

catapult (n): A military machine for hurling missiles, such as large stones or spears, used in medieval times

cathedral (n): The main church of a bishop's see, containing the cathedra or the bishop's throne *

chausses (n): The forerunner of trousers. They consisted of two pant legs, which weren't necessarily joined

chivalry (n): The characteristics of a Feudal knight: courage, courtesy, nobility, fairness, respect for women, protection of the poor. **chivalrous** (adj): He behaved in a chivalrous manner. * **C**

churl (n): A member of the lowest order of freemen; an ill-bred person. **churlish** (adj): Rude, ill-mannered. He is a churlish person.

crossbow (n): Weapon used by an archer

crusade (n): Any of the military expeditions which Christians undertook from the end of the 11th to the end of the 13th Centuries to recover the Holy Land from the Moslems; a vigorous, concerted action for some cause or idea, or against some abuse. She went on a crusade against teenage drinking. **C**

dunce (n): A dolt, a stupid person, from a schoolman, Duns Scotus, of the Medieval Ages, who was an opponent to progress, hence a dunce, who wore a tall, pointed dunce cap.

famine (n): An acute or general shortage of food; the time of this **C**

fealty (n): Solemn oath between a vassal and his liege, pledging service in return for protection

flying buttress (n): An arch developed in the Middle Ages to extend a Gothic-style building to brace part of it, seen most often on cathedrals

fostering (n): Sending children to live with friends, relatives, or political allies to learn necessary social skills, rather like boarding school

gargoyle (n): A roof spout carved to represent a grotesque human or animal figure, found on Gothic buildings

gossipry (n): Choosing Godparents for children; a way to cement alliances, as children were often fostered to their Godparents, which created lasting ties between households

guild (n): A union of men in the same craft or trade for mutual promotion of common interests

heraldry (n): Science of creating, recording, and reading Coats of Arms which identified members of the nobility

humors (n): Four body fluids which were believed to govern an individual's health and personality: Blood, phlegm, black bile, and yellow bile

joust (n): A combat between two mounted knights or men-at-arms using lances; a tilting match. (v) To engage in mounted combat with lances

knight (n): A medieval gentleman-soldier, usually high-born, raised by a sovereign to privileged military status after training as a page and squire *

masterpiece (n): The greatest work made or done by a person or group. The *Mona Lisa* is thought to be Leonardo da Vinci's greatest work.

monastery (n): Community in which monks live

page (n): A young person in the process of learning social etiquette by waiting on his/her elders

peasant (n): Person of lowest class

pilgrim (n): A wanderer; one who travels to a holy place. **pilgrimage** (n): A journey to a holy place

plague (n): A contagious, epidemic disease that is deadly; anything that troubles. Insects are often the source of plagues. Rats with infected fleas carried the plague in the Middle Ages.

psalm (n): A sacred song or poem. **psalter** (n): A book containing same *

plate (n): Armor composed of several, over-lapping or connected sections of metal, shaped to the wearer's body

serf (n): A slave bound to his master's land and transferred with it to a new owner

shield (n): A broad piece of armor made of rigid material and strapped to the arm or carried in the hand for protection against hurled or thrust weapons; a person or thing that provides protection; (v): To keep safe from danger, attack, or harm

sojourn (n & v): A brief or temporary stay, visit. **sojourner** (n): A traveler

tapestry (n): A heavy cloth woven with rich, often varicolored designs or scenes, usually hung on walls for decoration or used to cover furniture.

tournament (n): A medieval martial sport in which two groups of mounted and armored combatants fought against each other with blunted lances or swords. Any competition or test of opposing wills likened to the sport in which knights fought with lances

trencher (n): Horizontal slice of bread used as a plate. If you weren't too hungry, your uneaten trencher would be collected and given as alms to the poor.

yeoman (n): An attendant or man

Measures Used During Middle Ages And Later

Admiralty mile: A former British unit of length equivalent to 6,080 feet (1,853.184 meters); 800 feet longer than a statute mile

ångstrom = 1.0×10^{-10} meters. Originally it was the length of a bar of metal held in Paris. Astronomers use it as a unit of measure equal to 1 hundred-millionth of a centimeter. Today, this is a very high-tech word. See detailed information in encyclopedias or online at Wikipedia

arpent: Any of various French units of land measurement, especially one used in parts of Canada and the southern United States and equal to about 0.4 hectare (0.85 acre). **etymology**: French, from Old French, from Latin *arepennis*, half acre.

bolt: 40 yards; 32 ells for measurement of cloth

chain: An instrument used in surveying and measuring land, consisting of 100 linked pieces of iron or steel and measuring 66 feet (20.1 meters), also called

Charlemagne's foot: The official standard by which a foot was measured

cubit = 45.72 centimeters: An ancient unit of linear measure, from the elbow to the tip of the longest finger of a man, or about **1 cubit** = 18± - 22± inches, **46 centimeters±**, although that varies with the height of the man doing the measurement. There is also a "long" cubit that is longer than a regular cubit by a handbreadth. (Ezekiel 43:13) One of the earliest records of precise measurement is from Egypt. The Egyptians studied the science of geometry to assist them in the construction of the Pyramids. It is believed that about 3000 years BC, the Egyptian unit of length came into being.

The "**Royal Egyptian Cubit**" was decreed to be equal to the length of the forearm from the bent elbow to the tip of the extended middle finger plus the width of the palm of the hand of the pharaoh or king ruling then. "**Royal Cubit Master**" was carved out of a block of granite to endure for all times. Workers engaged in building tombs, temples, pyramids, etc., were supplied with cubits made of wood or granite. The Royal Architect or Foreman of the construction site was responsible for maintaining and transferring the unit of length to workers' instruments.

They were required to bring back their cubit sticks at each full moon to be compared to the Royal Cubit Master. Failure to do so was punishable by death. Though the punishment prescribed was severe, the Egyptians had anticipated the sprit of the present day system of legal metrology, standards, traceability, and calibration recall.

With this standardization and uniformity of length, the Egyptians achieved surprising accuracy. Thousands of workers were engaged in building the Great Pyramid of Giza. Through the use of cubit sticks, they achieved an accuracy of 0.05%. In roughly 756 feet or 9,069.4 inches, they were within 4 1/2 inches. (See http://en.wikipedia.org/wiki/Cubit for more information.)

digit: The breadth of one finger. How many of your digits equals an inch? A foot?

ell: An obsolete English linear measure equal to 45 inches (114 cms). Take a male adult of roughly average size. Measure the distance from his shoulder to his wrist. You should find that it is about 22–23 inches (56–58 cm). That's one of the oldest ways to define an *ell*, once the usual measure in many parts of Europe for textiles such as woolen cloth. It was considered to be roughly equal to six hand-breadths — a hand was 4 inches, **a unit still used for measuring the heights of horses**, which would make an *ell* about 24 inches.

In Old English, *ell* meant the arm, so that the *elbow* is the arm bend. There was even a saying *give him an inch and he will take an ell*; when the ell was replaced by the yard, the saying changed, too. In the Medieval period in England, the **ell** was fixed in size by various acts of Parliament to be 45 inches—twice the size of the older unit. Even this is open to some variation, as the same acts of Parliament defined an inch to be the breadth of the thumb, in particular that of the official, the *alnager*, whose job it was to measure and stamp each piece of cloth, a key English export of the period, as conforming to the law.

His name comes from Old French *aulne*, to measure by the ell, a word which has the same Indo-European root as Latin *ulna*, the forearm. The *alnager*, whose job was to protect buyers of woolen cloth from fraud, was an important part of medieval consumer protection.

finger: The of a finger used as a linear measure

foot: The popular belief is that the original standard was the length of a man's foot. Some believe that the original measurement of the English foot was from King Henry I, who had a foot 12-inches long.

Gunter's chain: Ordinarily used in measuring land, consisting of 100 linked pieces of iron or steel and measuring 66 feet (1 *rod.* 20.1 meters)

hectare (Ha): A measure of area, or superficies (outer surface of an area), containing a hundred acres, or 10,000 square feet

inch: 3 grains of barley lined up end to end; width of a man's thumb

King Henry I = a yard from tip of his nose to outstretched thumb. Can you imagine someone in the year 1010 A.D. requesting a King Henry I blanket?

league: An obsolete unit of length of an hour's walk, usually equal to three miles (4.8 kilometers) and used as a land measure chiefly on the continent of Europe. The Roman league, however, was half this length, or 1.5 Roman miles (7500 Roman feet or 2.22 km). See *Charge of the Light Brigade* by Alfred Tennyson on page 53. The marine league of England and the United States is equal to three marine, or geographical, miles of 6080 feet each.

micron: A unit of length equal to one millionth of a meter or the thousandth part of one millimeter. It is no longer in technical use.

mil: A unit of length equal to one thousandth of an inch; used to specify thickness, for example, of sheets or wire

milestone: A stone marker set up on a roadside to indicate the distance in miles from a stated point

nail: A former unit of length for cloth equal to 1/16 of a yard

pace: A unit of length equal to 3 feet; defined as 91.44 centimeters; originally taken to be the average length of a stride; 5 Roman feet: 58 inches.

palm: A unit of length equal to either the width or the length of the hand from the wrist to the ends of the fingers. (See http://en.wikipedia.org/wiki/Cubit for more information.)

perch: A linear measure of 16.5 feet

pica: A linear unit (1/6 inch) used in printing

pole: A linear measure of 16.5 feet

pygmy: From *pygme*, a Greek unit of length, equal to the distance between a man's elbow and his knuckles (about 13 1/2 inches.

rod: 22 yards / 66 feet / 25 links /1 *chain*

rood: A measure of five and a half yards in length; a red; a perch; a pole.

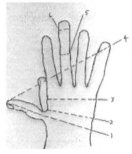

span: The distance from the tip of the thumb to the tip of the little finger when the hand is fully extended, formerly used as a unit of measure equal to about 9 in/23 cms

stadia: 3 miles ±

stere: A unit of cubic measure in the metric system, being a cubic meter, or **stere** kiloliter, and equal to 35.3 cubic feet, or nearly 1/ cubic yards.

Probe and Shed Light

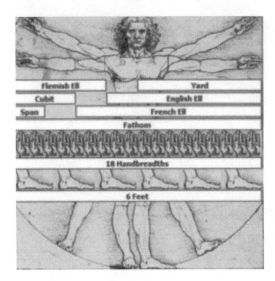

This derivation of the **Vitruvian Man** by Leonardo da Vinci depicts nine historical units of measurement: The **Yard**, the **Span**, the **Cubit**, the Flemish **Ell**, the English **Ell**, the French **Ell**, the **Fathom**, the **Hand**, the **Foot**. The Vitruvian man was drawn to scale, so the units depicted are displayed with their proper historical ratios.

http://www.baronage.co.uk/bphtm-02/moa-10.html
http://www.hemyockcastle.co.uk/measure.htm

Fibonacci, was an Italian mathematician, considered by some "the most talented mathematician of the Middle Ages. "Find the **Fibonacci sequence** and other advanced fun with numbers in the Appendix, page 229.

E. **Vikings** were active during the Middle Ages, but the material is so profuse and the interest of students so intense, that I suggest the Middle/Medieval ages and the Vikings be taught separately.

a. Literature

1. sagas
2. Norse mythology
3. *The Challenge of Thor* by Henry Wadsworth Longfellow

b. Films from Danish embassy

c. Geography

   1. L'Anse aux Meadows: Only proven Viking settlement in the New World
   2. Use atlases or maps of Denmark, Norway, Sweden, Scotland, and England to locate Viking settlements in Europe and England by looking for these place name endings:

      a. -beck = brook: Rhinebeck
      b. -by = village: Ashby, Barnby, Risby
      c. -chester, caster: Lancaster
      c. -set = mountain pasture or shielding: Summerset
      d. -worth = farm: Kenilworth

   3. Look also for these names:

      a. Berg: rock, small mountain
      b. Borg (borough): castle, fortified town
      c. Dal (-dale): valley
      d. Fjell (-fell), mountain
      e. Gård (garth), farm
      f. Nes (ness), headland, promontory
      g. Øy (ey), island
      h. Sund (sound), strait(s)
      i. Torp /Thorpe: a secondary settlement, outlying farm
      j. Våg (voe), bay
      k. Vik (wick), bay

d. English words from the Vikings:

   1. **Wednesday**: Odin / Woden's Day
   2. **Thursday**: Thor's Day
   3. **Friday**: Freya / Frigga's Day

e. **Interdisciplinary Guide to the Vikings:** This 10-page illustrated guide includes details for advance planning and preparations; bibliography of literature; suggestions for writing, art, music, geography, math, science and physical education activities; names from Norse mythology; *The Challenge of Thor* by Henry Wadsworth Longfellow; suggestions for

speakers, field trips, audio-visual aids and enriching pursuits; spelling challenges; comprehensive bibliography of resources;
*Available at www.seepub.com

f. **Vocabulary**

berserk (adj & adv): In or into a state of violent rage; from Norse legend, a warrior who worked himself into a frenzy before a battle. He must have been berserk when he shot his friend. *

bow / prow (n): The front of any boat. The Vikings often had carved figures on the bows of their ships. (See stern below.)

-chester / -caster: Suffix meaning camp. Westchester would therefore mean "west camp." **C**

fiord (n): A narrow inlet of the sea, between high banks or rocks, as on the coasts of Norway and Alaska *

geyser (n): A natural hot spring that throws out a spray of steam and water now and then. The Vikings were <u>enthralled</u> by the geysers in Iceland. *

rune (n): Mystery or magic. Any of the characters of an alphabet used by Scandinavians and Germanic peoples; something inscribed or written in such characters; any similar character or mark having some mysterious meaning or magical powers attributed to it

saga (n): A long Scandinavian adventure story of the Middle Ages, telling about historical or legendary heroes, families, deeds, and events; any long history or tale

stern: (n): The rear part of a ship or boat (See bow/prow above.)

thrall (n): A slave. **enthrall** (v): To make a slave of. Children enthralled by television could be said to be slaves of it.

F. **Ireland and Scotland (ancient and modern)**

a. Literature: folk / fairy tales
b. Art: make decorations for banquet tables (see "k" below)
c. Music: *Tristan and Isolde*, harp
d. Physical education: Irish dancing

e. Activities
   1. learn Irish dancing (invite local instructor)
   2. count in Gaelic from 1 to 10:

      1: aon (AY-un)
      2: do (DHOH)
      3: tri (TREE)
      4: ceathair (CA-her)
      5: cuig (KOO-ig)
      6: se (SHAY)
      7: seacht (SHOCT)
      8: ocht (OCT)
      9: aoi (NEE)
      10: deich (JEH)

   3. read, write, and learn limericks

   4. Hold a banquet

      a. Invite a harpist to play during dinner.
      b. Perform Irish dancing.
      c. Make Irish stew and soda bread.

   5. Vocabulary

angler (n): A fisherman. Many Irish and Scottish people are ardent anglers.

argyle (adj): A diamond pattern with criss-crossing stripes. He wore an argyle sweater. *

black sheep (n): A rascal or trickish person; the one who is different. She was the black sheep of the family. **C**

blarney (n): Flattery; a way of coaxing someone with exaggerated compliments. He's full of blarney!

brogue (n): The pronunciation of English as spoken by the Irish. She has a lovely brogue. *

clan (n): An early form of a social group, as in the Scottish Highlands, composed of several families claiming descent from a common ancestor. They belong to the Clan MacDougal.

collier (n): A coal miner *

emerald (adj): A shade of green, taken from the color of the gem. Ireland is often called the Emerald Isle.

firth (n): A narrow inlet or arm of the sea, used especially in Scotland. He sailed on the Firth of (the river) Forth.

glen (n): A mountain valley; a narrow, secluded valley. Ireland and Scotland have many glens.

heather (n): A low-growing plant with stalks of small, bell-shaped, purplish-pink flowers, esp. in the British Isles

hooligan (n): Idiom from an Irish family in London known for its rowdiness; similar to ruffian or hoodlum. Don't act like a hooligan!

limerick (n): A nonsense poem of five lines, with the rhyme scheme AABBA. "There once was a man from ..." *

> There was a young fellow named Hall
> Who fell in the spring in the fall
> 'Twould have been a sad thing
> Had he died in the spring
> But he didn't; he died in the fall.

loch (n): A lake. In Scotland, Loch Ness is known for its alleged monster; Loch Lomond figures in a well-known Scotch song.

lozenge (n): A plane figure with four equal sides and two obtuse angles; a diamond. A shape often found in Celtic designs. Why are some cough drops called lozenges? * **C**

Mc, Mac: Surname prefix meaning "son of" in Irish and Scottish families: McDonald, MacDonald

paisley (adj): A pattern characterized by scroll-shaped designs in it, originally made in Paisley, Scotland *

spud (n): An acronym for the **S**ociety for the **P**reservation of an **U**nwholesome **D**iet. The society was formed in the 1700's in England to ban the eating of potatoes.

steeplechase (n): A cross-country horse race with many obstacles toward a distant steeple; popular in Ireland

tartan / plaid (adj): Cloth with a design of lines and squares, originally woolen **C**

verdant (adj): Green color in nature. Irish hills are verdant. **verdure** (n): Greenness. Verdure covered the hillside. **C**

wake (n): A watch kept over a dead person

G. China/Japan (Old World)

1. Literature: *Sadako and the Thousand Paper Cranes* by Eleanor Cocrr; http://www.sadako.com has a video on how to fold a paper crane, as well as fairy tales and folk tales
2. Art: Calligraphy of Chinese characters; seals and insignias
3. Dragons
4. Paper lanterns
5. Origami
6. Tanabata decorations
7. Kites
8. Science: pandas, koi (fish)
9. Physical education: volleyball, ping-pong
10. Activities:

   a. Celebrate Chinese New Year (get materials from Chinese restaurants).
   b. Lunch at a Chinese restaurant.
   c. Prepare Chinese meal with seaweed soup and rice.
   d. Learn about and prepare tea ceremony.
   e. Hold koi / goldfish festival.
   f. Collect items from home that say "Made in China /Japan".
   g. Eat sushi.

11. Speakers: karate & judo instructors; Oriental parents and friends
12. Challenges: spell countries' cities.

Probe and Shed Light

13. Field trips: art and history museums
14. Vocabulary

amuck / amok (adj & adv): In a frenzy. **run amuck**: To rush about in a frenzy to kill; to lose control of oneself and do, or attempt, violence

imperial (adj): Of an empire; having the rank of an emperor or empress; having supreme authority. We visited the Imperial Palace in Beijing. They bowed to their Imperial Majesties.

kimono (n): A loose outer garment with short, wide sleeves and a sash, worn by both men and women in Japan

kowtow (n & v): The act of kneeling and touching the ground with the forehead to show great or submissive respect; a Chinese form of greeting to a superior. Everyone kowtowed to the boss.

H. Africa, India, and The Middle East
1. Literature: folk / fairy tales / novels / biographies
2. Art: masks, table decorations for culminating meal
3. Music: native instruments / songs / dances
4. Geography: outline maps
5. Native clothing
6. Physical education: games, dances
7. Activities: feast or banquet with ethnic foods, table decorations
8. Vocabulary

afghan (n): A crocheted or knitted soft wool blanket or shawl which originated in the Near East   *

arid (adj): Dry land. Parts of Africa and India are often extremely arid. **C**

bazaar (n): A market place, especially in the Middle East * **C**

cashmere (n & adj): Fine wool found beneath the hair of the goats of Kashmir, India; clothing made of that wool   *

damask (adj): A reversible figured fabric commonly used for tablecloths and draperies. I bought damask napkins to match our tablecloth.

drought (n): Absence of moisture, especially of rainfall. When there is a drought, land is *arid*. * **C**

famine (n): An acute and general shortage of food; the time of this. India and Africa experience many famines. * **C**

khaki (adj): Dull yellowish brown; cloth that is khaki colored, from a Hindu word meaning dust or dust-colored. Military uniforms are often khaki * **C**

monsoon (n): The rainy season of southwest India; a periodic wind, especially in the Indian Ocean and southern Asia. The monsoon freshened the *arid* land and filled the lakes and rivers. **C**

populous (adj): Full of people; thickly inhabited. New Delhi is a populous place.

Sanskrit (n): Any written form of old Indic literary language dating from the 3d century, still used in the ritual of the Northern Buddhist Church

sari (n): The principal outer garment of a Hindu woman, consisting of a long piece of cloth worn wrapped around the body with one end over the head * **C**

subcontinent (n): Not as large as a whole continent. India is a subcontinent. **C**

Taj Mahal (n): A large, imposing marble tomb (mausoleum) built in 1631-45 at Agra, India, by an emperor in memory of his favorite wife

veldt/ veld (n): In South Africa, open grassy country with almost no trees

See also: agrarian, delta, nomad, peninsula, rural and urban under other headings.

I. **Explorers**: Old World and New World; Pirates; Boats
    Explorers searched for new land in the hopes of finding spices; pirates hoped to prey on those who had been successful

    1. Those who went east from Europe: Marco Polo, Henry the Navigator

    2. Those who went west from Europe: Columbus, Magellan, Drake

    3. Interesting topics:

Probe and Shed Light

     a.   Pirates
     b.   Spices

4. Poetry challenges:

CAPTAIN KIDD
(1650 (?) - 1701
by Stephen Vincent Benet

This person in the gaudy clothes
Is worthy Captain Kidd.
They say he never buried gold.
I think, perhaps, he did.

The say it's all a story that
His favorite little song
Was "Make these lubbers walk the plank!"
I think, perhaps, they're wrong.

They say he never pirated
Beneath the Skull-and-bones.
He merely traveled for his health
And spoke in soothing tones.
In fact, you'll read in nearly all
The newer history books
That he was mild as cottage cheese

CONQUISTADOR
by Elizabeth Coatsworth

Let it be understood that I am Don Juan Gomez!
My blood is pure blood from the proudest blood of Spain
And I own hills and valleys beyond a wide day's riding
And heavy lies the silver upon my bridle rein.

Let it be understood that I am Don Juan Gomez!
My saddle cloth is fringed with scalps of Indians I have slain,
And when I see a girl whom I may wish in marriage
I shall demand but once, and need not ask again.

Let it be understood that I am Don Juan Gomez!
Only in prayer to bend the knee and bow the head I deign,
And when I pray, the saints go hurrying to the Virgin
And cry, "Don Juan is praying, and must not pray in vain!"

5. Vocabulary

Barbary Coast (n): The coastal region in northern Africa; the Moslem countries of Morocco, Algiers, Tunis, and Tripoli; centers of piracy **C**

booty (n): Goods taken from the enemy; plunder; pillage. The pirates shared their booty with all hands.

Bounding Main (n): The ocean. The pirates sailed up and down the Bounding Main.

buccaneer (n): A pirate or sea robber *

caravan (n): A company of travelers, especially of merchants or pilgrims traveling together for safety **C**

chandler (n): A retailer of supplies and groceries. A ship chandler sells provisions for ships.

corsair (n): A pirate, a privateer, especially of the Barbary Coast

doldrums (n): The dead calms and light, fluctuating winds of certain equatorial ocean regions. They spent days caught in the doldrums.

freebooter (n): A plunderer, a pirate, a *buccaneer*

galley (n): The kitchen on a ship

loot (n): *Booty* taken from another. (v) To rob

mutiny (n & v): Rebellion of sailors against their officers. To rebel against authority

oasis (n): A fertile place in the desert due to the presence of water; any fertile place in the midst of waste or a quiet place in the midst of noise **C**

plunder (n): Goods taken by force. (v): To rob by force

Probe and Shed Light

port (n): The port side of a ship is the left side. To turn a ship to port is to turn left.

sea dog (n): A sailor, especially an experienced one

starboard (n): The right side of a ship; opposite of *port* **C**

stern (n): The back end of a boat

swarthy (adj): Having a dark skin. The *sea dog* was swarthy.

swashbuckler (n): A blustering, swaggering, fighting man

tempest (n): A storm. The tempest turned the ship to port.

Timbuktu (n): A West African city on the Niger River through which explorers and Eastern traders often passed. Used today to mean a far-off place. She might as well be in Timbuktu for all the good she'll do us! **C**

See also barter, bow & prow, stern, wright
http://www.castlemoyle.com/

J.   Native Americans

1.   POEMS
a.   An Indian Prayer

> O' GREAT SPIRIT, whose voice I hear in the winds,
> And whose breath gives life to all the world, hear me!
> I am small and weak; I need your
> strength and wisdom.
>
> Let Me Walk In Beauty, and make my eyes
> ever behold the red and purple sunset.
>
> Make My Hands
> respect the things you have made and my ears sharp
> to hear your voice.
>
> Make Me Wise so that I may understand
> the things you have taught my people.

Let Me Learn the lessons you have
hidden in every leaf and rock.

I Seek Strength, not to be greater than
my brother, but to fight my greatest enemy - myself.

Make Me Always Ready to come with
clean hands and straight eyes.

So When Life Fades, as the fading
sunset, my sprit may come to you
without shame.

b.   A Chief Of The Desert

(Navajo Poem)

It was the wind that gave them life.
It is the wind that comes out of our
 mouths now that gives us life.
When this ceases to blow we die.
In the skin at the tips of our fingers
we see the trail of the wind;
It shows us where the wind blew
when our ancestors were created.

2.   Spelling of tribes' names: See below
3.   Foods: maize, sunflower, wild
4.   Words in common English usage
5.   Activity books from many publishers
6.   Literature: legends
7.   Music
8.   Art: pottery, weaving, beadwork, cave art, copper jewelry, model of a cliff
     dwelling; have children bring family's turquoise pieces to class
9.   Medicine
10. Environment and lifestyles: desert, prairie, swamps
11. Dances
12. Tools: tomahawk, bow & arrows, knives for canoe making

13. Tribes: Assign a student or two to research each of these tribes: Where they once lived; where they live today. How many cities, counties, rivers, parks, parkways, etc., can students find as in the examples below? Use their names as spelling challenges.

> Algonquin (Park in NY)
> Apache
> Blackfeet
> Cherokee
> Cheyenne (Wyoming)
> Chinook
> Choctaw (County, Oklahoma)
> Comanche (County, Oklahoma)
> Delaware (State and river)
> Hopi
> Iroquois
> Mohawk (New York)
> Navajo
> Nisqualli
> Pawnee (Oklahoma)
> Seminole (Oklahoma)
> Sioux (City, Iowa; Falls, South Dakota)
> Taos (New Mexico
> Tlingit
> Zuni

14. Vocabulary

adobe (n): A sun-dried, unburned brick of clay and straw; a structure built with this type of brick **C**

tepee (n): A portable dwelling of certain Native American peoples, especially on the Great Plains, consisting of a conical framework of poles covered with skins or bark

tomahawk (n): A light ax formerly used as a tool or weapon by some Native American peoples, a similar implement or weapon

turquoise (n): A blue to blue-green mineral of aluminum and copper, prized as a gemstone in its polished blue form. (adj) The color of the mineral **C**

prairie (n): An extensive area of flat or rolling, predominantly treeless, grassland, especially the large tract or plain of central North America **C**

K. Latin America: Mayas, Aztecs, Incas

1. **Words common to all:**
   a. **agrarian** (adj): Relating to agricultural or rural matters * C
   b. **deity**: A god
   c. **maize** (n): Corn *
   d. **quesadilla:** A toasted tortilla with melted cheese inside (pronounced kay sa dee´ uh) *
   e. **tortilla:** A type of thin, unleavened flat bread, made from finely ground maize (corn) or wheat flour * (pronounced tor tee´ uh)

2. **Mayas**

   a. **Cenote** (n): A water-filled limestone sinkhole of the Yucatán *
   b. **Chiapas:** The southernmost state of Mexico, located towards the southeast of the country
   c. **Chichen Itza:** A major regional center in the northern Maya lowlands on the *Yucután peninsula*
   d. **Guatemala:** A country of northern Central America. The site of a Mayan civilization dating back to 1500 BC, conquered by Spain in 1524 *
   e. **Kukulcan:** The Mayan supreme god; related to Quetzalcoatl (see under Aztecs) *
   f. **Palenque:** An important Maya archeological site in the Mexican state of *Chiapas*
   g. **Pok-ta-pok** (n): Ballgame of the Maya *
   h. **Tikal:** The largest of the ruined cities of the Maya civilization
   i. **Yucután Peninsula:** Located in Southeast Mexico *

3. **Incas**

   a. **alpaca:** A domesticated South American mammal related to the llama and having fine, long wool

b. **Cuzco**: City in southeastern Peru, high in the Andes Mountains, Capital of the Inca Empire

c. **Ecuador**: South American country that straddles the equator and is bordered by Colombia on the north, Peru on the east and south, and by the Pacific Ocean on the west. The country also includes the Galápagos Islands about 600-miles west of the mainland.

d. **guanaco**: Animal related to the llama

e. **guano**: A substance composed chiefly of the dung (excrement of animals) of sea birds or bats, accumulated along certain coastal areas or in caves, and used as fertilize *

f. **Lake Titicaca**: The highest navigable lake on earth at 12,580 feet altitude. It straddles the border between Peru and Bolivia. *

g. **llama**: A domesticated South American ruminant mammal related to the camel, raised for its soft, fleecy wool, and used as a beast of burden. Pronounced *lama* or *yama.* *

h. **Machu Picchu**: A pre-Columbian Incan site, rediscovered in 1911 by Yale archaeologist Hiram Bingham, is one of the most beautiful and enigmatic sites in the world. *

i. **quipu**: A system of knotted cords used by the Incas in the Andean region to store massive amounts of information important to their culture and civilization *

4. **Aztecs**: A civilization living in Mexico when the Spaniards arrived in 1519

a. **Aztec calendar**: The **Aztec** sun calendar is a circular stone with pictures representing how the Aztecs measured days, months, and cosmic cycles

b. **Hieroglyphics**: A system of writing in which pictorial symbols represent meaning or sounds or a combination of meaning and sound *

c. **Huitzilopochtli**: The Aztec sun and war god, whose name means "Blue Hummingbird on the Left (south)", the warrior soul from paradise *

d. **Montezuma**: In 1502, **Montezuma II** became the ninth Aztec emperor. *

e. **Popocatépetl**: A snow-capped volcano that stands 13,776 ft. (4200 m) above the surrounding basin, the second highest peak in Mexico. It is often referred to as El Popo and means "Smoking Mountain."*

f. **Quetzalcoatl**: In Aztec religion, considered a leader among the deities, often referred to as the feathered serpent god. The name is a combination of quetzal, a brightly colored American bird, and coatl, meaning serpent. *

g. **Tenochtitlan**: The Aztecs' capital city was built in the center of enormous Lake Texcoco. Today its remains lie beneath the foundations of Mexico City. *

h. **Teotihuacán**: The largest pre-Columbian city in the Americas, today located 40 km (about 24.8 miles) northeast of Mexico City

(**See also:** artifact, hieroglyphics, pre-Columbian, shard and taboo under General Ancient Cultures.)

References:
Mathematical Contributions of the Mayas, Aztecs & Incas: A Native American Curriculum Unit for Middle & High School
http://www.hemyockcastle.co.uk/measure.htm
http://touregypt.net/featurestories/measures.htm

G. **Publishing Companies for History, Science and Social Studies** (Those with an * I found to be of high quality).

*Bellerophon (great coloring books, records, and ancient cultures posters): PO Box 21307, Santa Barbara CA 93121; (800) 253-9943; www.bellerophonbooks.com/

Boston Fine Arts Museum (games, educational materials): P.O. Box 244, Avon, MA 02322-0244; www.mfa.org/shop; (800) 225-5592;

*Cobblestone Publishing Company produces theme-based magazines covering American history (Cobblestone), cultures and geography (Faces), world history (Calliope), science and space (Odyssey), African American history (Footsteps), general social studies/ reading (Appleseeds), and archaeology (Dig): 30 Grove Street, Suite C, Peterborough, NH 03458; 800-821-0115; http://cobblestonepub.com/index.html;customerservice@ caruspub.com; 1-800-821-0115

*Dover Publications, Inc. (coloring books, stickers, punch-out and cut-and-make books, masks and other materials): 31 East 2nd Street, Mineola, NY 11501; www.doverpublishing.com/

*EDC Publishing/ Usborne): 10302 E. 55th Place, Tulsa, OK 74146; edc@edcpub.com; (800) 475-4522 http://www.edcpub.com/corp/

Educational Resources: (great software); 1550 Executive Drive Elgin, Il 60123; http://www.edresources.com/; (800) 860-7004

MacDonald Publishing (posters) 567 Hanley Industrial Ct. St. Louis, MO 63144; 800-722-8080

Metropolitan Museum of Art (games, educational materials):   255 Gracie Station, New York, NY 10028; www.metmuseum.org/; (800) 468-7386

Milliken (overhead projector transparencies and workbooks): 11643 Lilburn Park Road, St. Louis, MO 63146; www.millikenpub.com/; (800) 325-4136;

Modern Curriculum Press/Pearson Learning Group/Dale Seymour Press/ Celebration Press http://plgcatalog.pearson.com/co_home. cfm?site_id=12; (800) 321-3106

*Owl Magazine, The Discovery Magazine for Children: Bayard, The Owl Group, 49 Front Street East, Toronto, M5E 1B3, Ontario, Canada; www.owlkids.com/; magazines@indas.on.ca; 1-800-551-6957

Perfection Learning (pre-K - adult books: literature, multicultural materials, blank maps of regions of the world): 1000 North Second Avenue, Logan, IA 51546-1099; http://www.perfectionlearning.com; (800) 831-4190. Perfection does great **book fairs**.

*Ranger Rick (children's nature magazine): National Wildlife Foundation, 11100 Wildlife Center Dr, Reston, VA 20190; 800-822-9919; http:// www.nwf.org/kids/

*S & S Arts & Crafts (project materials to support science and social studies; some in classroom kits, including Ancient Culture Design Posters and learning walls, 48"x72"): P.O. Box 513, Colchester, CT 06415-0513; (800) 243-9232; http://www.ssww.com/

Scholastic News (classroom magazines and books) (800) 807-2466 and Weekly Reader: 3001 Cindel Drive, Delren, NJ 08370; (800) 446-3355; http://www.scholastic.com/

*Social Studies School Service (catalogs for K-6 & 4-8; subject texts, teacher activity books, maps, learning center kits, videocassettes, computer software, eBooks,) 10200 Jefferson Blvd., P.O. Box 802, Culver City, CA 90232-0802; www.socialstudies.com/; (800) 421-4246

State Departments of Natural Resources: See local telephone listings.

Sundance (pre-K-8): P.O. Box 1326, Littleton, MA 01460; www.sundancepub.com; (800) 343-8204

US Government Printing Office, Washington, DC 20402; http://www.gpo.gov/

*Your Big Backyard (for children ages 3 to 9): National Wildlife Foundation, 11100 Wildlife Center Dr, Reston, VA 20190; 800-822-9919; http://www.nwf.org/

Zephyr Press: P.O. Box 66006, Tucson, AZ 8885728-6006. www.zephyrpress.com

*Zoobooks (individual subjects in magazine format, including most mammal species, snakes, insects, fish, etc.): Wildlife Education, Ltd., 12233 Thatcher Court, Poway, CA 92064; www.zoobooks.com; (800) 992-5034

Companies I haven't used but which have relevant materials: Frank Schaffer, Good Apple and Judy Instructo

ADDITIONAL REFERENCES FOR TEACHERS AND STUDENTS

http://history.about.com/with links to many subjects
http://www.education-world.com/history/
www.pbs.org/teachersource/soc_stud.htm
http://www.education-world.com/science
http://www.utexas.edu/utpress/subjects/legend.html
http://kids.discovery.com/
http://disney.go.com/index
http://www.howstuffworks.com/
http://www.kidwings.com/index.htm: About Owl Pellets
http://kids.nationalgeographic.com/
http://www.google.com/search?hl=en&q=kathy+schrock&aq=7&oq=KATHY

http://www.google.com/search?hl=en&q=time+for+kids&btnG=Search
http://www.dmoz.org/Kids_and_Teens/School_Time/Science/
http://pbskids.org/
http://www2.scholastic.com/browse/home.jsp
http://www.smithsonianeducation.org/
http://www.timeforkids.com/TFK/
http://kids.yahoo.com/
http://grammar.ccc.commnet.edu/grammar/

H. LEAVING HISTORICAL TIMES BEHIND, let's see what you can do with a United States' inauguration history quiz :

1. If you were president of the United States, what would you plan to accomplish during your first four years? Why?

2. If you were the wife or husband of the president, how would you spend your time?

3. Each student, or a group, draws one of the questions below, researches the answer, and reports to the class.

    a. Which multiple-term president holds the record for both the warmest January inauguration and the coldest?

        1. Franklin Delano Roosevelt
        2. Richard Nixon
        3. Ronald Reagan
        4. Bill Clinton

    b. Who contracted pneumonia after his one hour and 40 minute inaugural address and died one month into his administration?

        1. Franklin Pierce
        2. James K. Polk
        3. James Buchanan
        4. William Henry Harrison

    c. Which president took the oath of office aboard Air Force One?

        1. John F. Kennedy
        2. Richard Nixon
        3. Dwight Eisenhower
        4. Lyndon Johnson

d. **Who was the first president to ride in an automobile to his inauguration?**

    1. Woodrow Wilson
    2. Warren G. Harding
    4. Herbert Hoover
    5. Franklin Delano Roosevelt

e. **In his inaugural address, which president said,** "There are times when the future seems thick as a fog; you sit and wait, hoping the mists will lift and reveal the right path. But this is a time when the future seems a door you can walk right through to a room called tomorrow"?

    1. George Bush
    2. Bill Clinton
    3. Abraham Lincoln
    4. John F. Kennedy

f. **After a harsh and fractious election settled finally by the House of Representatives**, which president attempted to heal the national wounds by saying, "We are all Republicans. We are all Federalists."

    1. Abraham Lincoln
    2. Theodore Roosevelt
    3. Thomas Jefferson
    4. Ulysses S. Grant

g. **Which president's inaugural ball was reported to be so rowdy an affair that the new president was forced to escape the White House in secret?**

    1. Theodore Roosevelt
    2. John F. Kennedy
    3. Bill Clinton
    4. Andrew Jackson

h. Which president took the oath of office in Buffalo, N.Y.?

   1. Theodore Roosevelt
   2. Woodrow Wilson
   3. William McKinley
   4. Grover Cleveland

i. Whose inauguration was the first to be photographed?

   1. Abraham Lincoln
   2. James Buchanan
   3. Zachary Taylor
   4. Ulysses S. Grant

j. After winning the presidency by just more than 29,000 votes, who said in his inaugural address, "The best results in the operation of a government ... depend upon a proper limitation of purely partisan zeal"?

   1. John F. Kennedy
   2. Abraham Lincoln
   3. Thomas Jefferson
   4. Grover Cleveland

k. Presidents who were not elected: www.infoplease.com/spot/inaugural1.html

   Find answers at: http://www.washingtonpost.com/wpsrv/onpolitics/inauguration2001/quiz.htm

CHAPTER V

▼

CommuniCards®
AN ENGLISH-MATH COMBO

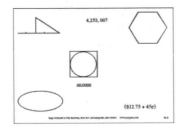

"The transformation of experience into concepts...
is the motive of language."
Suzanne K. Lanrer

When some of my seventh-grade students were unable to draw a line "about 2 inches long" or a circle with a one-inch diameter, I knew I had to find a way to get these important concepts into their heads. I finally hit on the idea of giving each student a card on which he was to draw a variety of geometric shapes and lines of varying lengths as instructed. It didn't take long for the whole class to get up to speed on these concepts. I continued to create other cards with directions that covered a wide range of topics.

A. CommuniCards˚ are quick and easy tools that:

1. Measure children's grasp of specific concepts in English and math

2. Advance students' abilities to express themselves in a clear and effective manner

3. Provide practice in giving logical and concise directions

4. Strengthen listening skills and abilities to follow directions

5. Advance acquisition of cognitive skills

6. Solidify understanding of spatial /directional words: right, left, up, down, above, below, next to, adjacent, clockwise, counter-clockwise, middle, center, corner, backwards, horizontal, vertical

7. Reinforce concepts in mathematics:

    a. Plus, minus
    b. Geometric shapes: Square, rhombus, rectangle, parallelogram, triangles, trapezoid, hexagon, circle, semi-circle
    c. Measurements, including length of lines in metric and American measures*
    d. Diameter, radius, bisect
    e. Size: As large as/about the size of…
    f. Roman numerals
    g. Characteristics of lines, shapes and angles: Bisect, parallel, diagonal, perpendicular, equilateral, elliptical, oval, acute, obtuse, and right angles

8. Reinforce concepts in English:

    a. Punctuation terms: Period, comma, colon, semicolon, apostrophe, open and close quotes, exclamation point, question mark, parentheses, brackets
    b. Upper and lower case
    c. Homonyms: Its, it's; to, two, too; their, there, they're; already, all ready; principle, principal, etc.
    d. Printed versus cursive letters
    e. Ampersand
    f. Dollar sign
    g. Spelling's worrisome words
    h. Analogies and creativity

9. Engage teachers and students in cooperative thinking tasks.

10. Teach participants to:

   a. Describe
   b. Question
   c. Seek alternatives
   d. Solve problems
   e. Be divergent in thinking
   f. Be creative
   g. Apply and extend knowledge

B. Putting CommuniCards Into Practice

1. One student, a recruit, stands in front of the others, and—with no advance preparation and using only verbal directions — describes everything, one by one, that is on the card he is holding. Those at their desks apply these directions to a paper the same size as the CommuniCard (1/4 of an 8" x 11" paper). When recruits do a perfect job, others' cards will look the same as theirs.

2. If a word is written on the card, the recruit presents it in a sentence. "Its. It's a hot day." (Class members write the sentence, spelling *its* however they think it should be.)

3. As the recruit proceeds, monitor how many and what kinds of questions participants ask in order to understand the directions. For example, if the recruit says, "Draw a circle," many hands will certainly shoot up. "How big a circle? Where does it go?" These questions cause the recruit to refine his approach. The ultimate answer would be, "Draw a circle about the size of quarter in the upper left corner of your card." A primary object of CommuniCards is to have students attain that type of fluency.

4. During the presentation, you should note how many "you knows" and "likes" the recruit uses, asking him to repeat what he said without the youthspeak. Also analyze the questions asked by participants as a measure of their comprehension. You should further recognize the particular concepts that need reinforcing. If an instruction such as, "Draw a line about 2 inches long" is misrepresented by some, then the concept of 2

inches needs more work. Encourage recruits to express measurements in both American and metric measures.*

5. After the presentation, participants hold up their "cards" for a comparison with the original. An analysis and discussion of variations will decide whether it was the fault of the presenter or the listener and will suggest ways for future improvement. Keep data not only of which cards each child presents but also of how the recruit and those in the class did with each card. This will help track everyone's proficiency. Also note areas of mild, medium, and great hesitation shown by the presenter, as well as displays of ingenuity and originality.

6. To be the most effective, CommuniCards should be presented at the rate of only one a day about two or three times a week. Allow 15 minutes per presentation and follow-up discussion. After each child has had his turn as being the presenter, allow a lapse of at least a month and then present these same cards again.

After everyone in the class has had a chance to present several CommuniCards from the classroom set, encourage them make their own cards for creative self-expression.

C. Assess CommuniCards' success by recording each child's fluency in presentations, thinking skills, and mastery of concepts, plus areas of others' weakness and progress.

You may purchase sets of each grades' cards at: http:www.seepub.com.

* Measurement provides a way to answer questions about "how many," "how much," and "how far." It is an indispensable component of business, manufacturing, art, medicine and many other aspects of daily life. We describe the sizes, capacities, and values of many things, and we select what instruments to use to determine the size of objects correctly. It is important for all of us to be able to use standard instruments including rulers, volume and capacity measures, timers, and emerging measurement technologies found in the home and workplace.

Probe and Shed Light

CHAPTER VI

▼

MEANINGFUL MATHEMATICS/ MASTERFUL MATH

*"One crucial goal of education is to rouse
and stimulate the love of mental adventure."*
Bertrand Russell

I. The Importance of Drill

Wherever I taught, I worked to increase children's speed and accuracy. I insisted on daily speed drills in adding, subtracting, multiplication, and division. When I had a choice, I used Holey Cards* (www.holeycards.com/ holeyCard). They have holes beneath each problem through which students write answers on a paper below. Despite occasional protests from students and parents, this type of regular drill is necessary, as it prepares students for work in algebra and higher math.

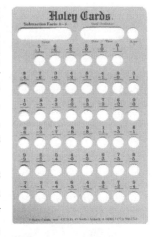

My days of teaching and tutoring algebra students taught me that most failing students weren't facile with basic facts. A student could work correctly all the way to the end of a problem with a result of, say, 6X = 48, and then write the answer as "7." Teachers with an overload of papers to correct do not have time to check through a student's work to see where or why he went wrong. If the answer isn't right, the teacher marks it with a big X. The student says, "See! I can't do 220algebra!" That is why I was relentless about having students start math classes with daily drills. I hope many of my students silently thanked me later when they did well in algebra!

Algebra, a science dealing with the logic of quantity and shape and arrangement of the branches of mathematics, and a study that develops the principles of mathematics for its own sake rather than for its immediate usefulness, has recently taken a new turn with public school educators. Many schools are now planning to require fifth graders to learn the basics of algebra. I oppose this idea. First of all, I don't believe the majority of students are ready for algebra at that age.

Secondly, I feel that students who lack innate mathematical abilities need not struggle needlessly with the laws of algebra but instead should take courses in practical math that will be useful for them in the future. Those students who absorb algebraic principles and continue to build on them as they pursue higher math will likely enter fields of science where this aptitude is necessary. It is especially interesting to note that many mathematicians and students who do well with various aspects of mathematics are often left-handed. Maybe there is a "math gene" after all!

Another problem with the standard math texts is the practice of presenting the metric system in one chapter <u>only</u>— but then never employ that method of measuring in those that follow. No wonder most Americans have a hard time utilizing metrics when needed! To counter this lack of continuous review, I substituted metrics for inches, feet, and yards in our texts' following chapters. Students should become facile with metrics since it is used in many countries and sciences.

I hope the many ways I found to improve children's abilities to attain mastery of important facts will be more pleasurable than ordinary drill. Perhaps I am in tune with Mark Twain, who said, *"I have never let my schooling interfere with my education."*

II. Basic Measures

A. Lengths/Linear Ranges

1. Go outside with a ruler that shows both metric and American measures. Help children become adroit in grasping various sizes, i.e., one meter is a little longer than 1 yard / 3 feet, which is also about half the height of a tall adult. A centimeter is more or less the diameter of a dime or a little less than half an inch. A millimeter is about the thickness of a dime. Have each estimate whether he walked one foot, two feet, 3 meters, or more. Then measure to see how close they came. Have them practice until they have a good understanding of various lengths.

2. **Use car trips** for children to estimate the distance they're planning to go, whether it's to the grocery store or a friend's house. How close were their guesses?

3. If you live or travel near Canada, have your children translate roadside metric distances into miles and vice versa.

B. **Linear Measures**: Help your children become comfortable with converting English to metric measures and visa-versa," i.e. "**5.5 yards = 1 rod**; 1 rod= 5.5 yards; **2 rods = 11 yards**; 11yards = 2 rods, etc.

METRIC	STANDARD/AMERICAN
10 millimeters = 1 centimeter	12 inches = 1 foot
10 centimeters = 1 decimeter	3 feet = 1 yard
10 decimeters = 1 meter	5 ½ yards = 1 rod
10 meters = 1 decameter	40 rods = 1 furlong/8th of a mile
10 decameters = 1 hectometer	8 furlongs = 1 statute mile

Metric-U.S. Measurement Conversions: http://www.easysurf.cc/menumt.htm

C. **Imaginary Linear Measurements**

1. **Longitude:** A line of longitude is a meridian and half of a great circle. In the sky, a **meridian** is an imaginary great circle on the celestial sphere. It passes through the north point on the horizon, through the celestial pole, up to the **zenith** (the direction pointing directly *above* a particular location), through the south point on the horizon, and through the **nadir** (the direction pointing directly *below* a particular location), and is perpendicular to the local horizon.

2. **Latitude**: Has the **equator** (see "d" below) as a natural starting position and gives the location of a place on Earth north or south of the equator. Lines of Latitude are the **horizontal** lines shown running east-to-west on maps. At which latitude do you live? Use an atlas to find your answer; look for the lines that appear straight and horizontal.

3. **Mason-Dixon Line**: A line between four U.S. states, forming part of the borders of Pennsylvania, Maryland, Delaware, and West Virginia (then part of Virginia). It was surveyed between 1763 and 1767 to determine the border between the free states and the slave states being disputed between British colonies in Colonial America. Popular speech uses the Mason-Dixon line symbolically as a cultural boundary between the Northern and the Southern United States (Dixie). This "line" got its name from Charles Mason and Jeremiah Dixon, the surveyors. Do you live above or below the Mason-Dixon line?

4. **Equator:** The **equator** divides the planet into a Northern Hemisphere and a Southern Hemisphere, and has a latitude of 0°. In which hemisphere do you live? How do you know?

D. Liquid Measures

1. Liquid measures

10 milliliters = 1 centiliter .... 2 gills = 1 cup
4 gills = 1 pint ....2 cups = 1 pint
10 centiliters = 1 cu. decimeter...................... 2 pints = 1 quart
10 decimeters = 1 liter............................... 4 quarts = 1 gallon
10 liters = 1 decaliter........................... 31 ½ gallons = 1 barrel
3 tsp= 1tbsp
4 tbsp = ¼ cup
16 tbsp = 1 cup

fifth: A quantity of liquor equal to one fifth of a United States gallon

gill: A United States liquid unit equal to 4 fluid ounces; a British imperial capacity unit (liquid or dry) equal to 5 fluid ounces or 142.066 cubic cms.

hogshead: A large cask especially one holding 63 gals (or 63-140 gallons)

jigger: A small glass adequate to hold a single swallow of whiskey

magnum: Latin, neuter of magnus great: A large wine bottle holding about 1.5 liters

Probe and Shed Light

pony: A small glass adequate to hold a single swallow of whiskey

2. **Dry Measures**

    bushel: A unit of volume equal to 4 pecks

> *"I love you, a bushel and a peck,*
> *A bushel and a peck, and a hug around the neck ..."*
> From *Guys and Dolls* musical

    cord: A unit of amount of wood cut for burning; 128 cubic feet

    dozen of anything = 12: A dozen eggs/balls/pictures; **half a dozen** = 6: Six eggs. *"Six of one and half a dozen of another."* An old saying meaning two things that are essentially the same and so there is no real choice to be made. **baker's dozen:** 13. One extra loaf to combat suspicion of short measure

    dry pint: A United States dry unit equal to 0.5 quart or 33.6 cubic in.

    gross=12 dozen=144. She bought a gross of nails.

    handful: As much or as many as the hand will grasp; a small quantity or number, as in a handful of people. Plural: handfuls.

    peck: One-fourth part of a bushel

A complete resource for more measures: http://www.easysurf.cc/cnver2.htm. Click on *Measurement Conversion Directory.*
http://www.iofm.net/community/kidscorner/maths/origin.htm

E. **Common abbreviations:**

    C = **hundred.** He gave me a C note, $100.
    K = **1,000.** k stands for kilo, as in kilogram, kilometer; also kg.
    M = million

F. **Weights**: Ounces to grams; pounds (lbs) to kilograms (14 pounds = 6.4 kilograms = 1 stone (British only); **kiloton**: A mass, 1000 tons (10,000 x 2000); **megaton**: A million tons

http://www.thefreedictionary.com/measurement
http://www.sosmath.com/algebra/unitconv/unit1/unit1.html
http://www.france-property-and information.com/quick metric_converter.htm
http://lamar.colostate.edu/~hillger/common.html
For metric quizzes, go to http://lamar.colostate.edu/~hillger/metric-week.html

G. Area

      144 sq. inches = 1 sq. foot
        9 sq. feet = 1 sq. yard
      30 ¼ sq. yards = 1 sq. rod
      160 sq. rods = 1 acre
      1 acre = 4,840 sq. yds

H. Time: See Appendix, page 230: *For the First Time in History, Time Mattered:* A complete document about time.

1.   Various lengths of times:
     a.   "jiffy" is an actual unit of time: 1/100th of a second.
     b.   60 seconds = 1 minute
     c.   60 minutes = 1 hour
     d.   A round in boxing: For men, 3 minutes; for women, 2 minutes
     e.   15 minutes = ¼ hour
     f.   30 minutes – ½ hour
     g.   45 minutes = ¾ hour
     h.   24 hours = 1 day
     i.   7 days = 1 week
     j.   30/31 days = 1 month, with the exception of February
     k.   360 days = 1 year
     l.   361 days = 1 leap year
     m.   12 months = 1 year
     n.   10 years=a decade. Ask children, according to their ages and abilities, to decide in which decade we are now living and the decades in which the following events took place:
          1. Their own birth
          2. Their grandmother's birth
          3. The US Revolutionary War
          4. The US Civil War
          5. Your own ideas _____

o. 10 decades=1 century; 100 years

p. 100 centuries=1000 years

q. 1000 years=1 millennium; a thousandth anniversary

r. 2000 years=2 millennia (note plural ending)

s. 1 light-year is a unit of length/distance that light can travel in one year, about 10 trillion km. More precisely, one light-year is equal to 9,500,000,000,000 kilometers and is used as a unit in expressing stellar distances. It is more than 63,000 times as great as the distance from the earth to the sun! Light moves at a velocity of about 300,000 kilometers (km) each second. So in one year, it can travel about 10 trillion km. More precisely, one light-year is equal to 9,500,000,000,000 kilometers. One light-year is 9.4605284×10^{15} meters or almost ten trillion kilometers and is the distance over which light can travel in a year's time. It is more than 63,000 times as great as the distance from the earth to the sun.

Why would anyone want such a big unit of distance? Well, on Earth, a kilometer may be just fine. It is a few hundred kilometers from New York City to Washington, DC; it is a few thousand kilometers from California to Maine. In the Universe, the kilometer is just too small to be useful. For example, the distance to the next nearest big galaxy, the Andromeda Galaxy, is 21 quintillion km (21,000,000,000,000,000,000 km.) This number is so large that it becomes hard to write and hard to interpret.

t. The rate of evolutionary change in a bird species wing, leg, or beak is assessed in units called darwins, which measure the proportional change in an organ over time. The changes over millions of years usually amount to one darwin or less. For detailed information on this measurement, go to: http://books. google.com/books?id=_dCrIwP85vkC&pg=PA53&lpg=PA53 &dq=darwin+measures&source=bl&ots

2. **Calculating time**

a. **Calendars**

1. **Prehistoric** inhabitants of the earth were skilled sky watchers who devised many ways of sighting and marking annual

astronomical evens, such as the summer and winter solstices and the spring and autumn equinoxes.

a. Kern Sun serpent in southern Ohio is one of two unique astronomical alignments that were used about 800 years ago by Native Americans to mark the summer and winter solstices.

b. The Maya believed that conditions for each date in the future repeat the conditions of some date in the past. The oldest such figure found in Maya records goes back four hundred million years! (See table for how the Maya wrote their numbers at http:// members.shaw.ca/mjfinley/astronomers.html.)

Use the Internet to find out more about these:

c. Stonehenge:

d. Avebury Ring: Use the Internet to find out more about this.

e. Easter Island: Use the Internet to find out more about this.

f. Aztecs: Use the Internet to find out more about these.

Which did you find the most interesting? Why?

2. **Historic**

a. Chinese: A system of chronology dating back to 27 B. C. 2009 is the Chinese year of the Ox and the year 4707.

b. Farmers' Almanacs

3. **Modern/Standard time**: November 18, 1883, the United States adopted standard time. Before then, people set their watches and clocks by the sun; when it was directly overhead, the time was 12 noon. With the adoption of standard time, the U.S. was divided into four time zones.

Reference: *Revolution in time: Clocks and the making of the Modern World* by David S. Landes.

b. **Chronologies**: The science that deals with the determination of dates and the sequence of events

1. Obsidian (the dating stone): Through the method of obsidian hydration measurement, the depth of water penetration on a surface of this stone reveals the dates of geologic and archaeologic events from the earliest cultural use of obsidian, through the Acheulian hand axes of East Africa, almost half a million years ago, to the end of the stone age in most of the New World. Less than half a thousand years in the past, traits of mankind's developing ways of life have been reflected in the use of obsidian.

2. Chrono-: Prefix and suffix meaning time
    a. synchronize: To occur at the same time; to operate in unison, as in swimming styles and traffic lights; people may synchronize their watches so that they are all set on the same time. I'm in synch with your ideas.

    b. asynchrony (without occurring at the same time), as in some music, bird eggs' hatching; asynchonous

    c. dendrochronology (wood + time study): Used for dating wood to reveal ages of barns, buildings, furniture, and other woods

    d. SYNCOM: **Syn**chronous **Com**muncation Satellite

    e. chronograph: Any of various instruments, as a stopwatch, for measuring and recording brief, precisely spaced intervals of time; a calendar watch

    f. chronological order: Events in the order in which they occur: school events; national holidays. Put your classmates' birthdays in chronological order. Name the wars in chronological order in which the U.S. has been involved.

    g. chronic: Of long duration; continuing; She is chronically late. She has a chronic cough; an illness. He is a chronic complainer.

h. chronobiology: Study of body clocks, including jet lag, also known as circadian desynchronosis

i. chronicle: A record of past events. Several newspapers use this as their name.

j. chronologies: The arrangement of events in time of occurrence. We can age trees by their rings, each ring indicating one year. We can do the same with some shells, coral, and sedimentary rocks.

k. anachronism: One that is out of its proper or chronological order, such as the contrail of an airplane in a Civil War film. Write a story from a picture, using at least one anachronism.

l. chronograms: A chronogram is a sentence or inscription in which specific letters (M,D,C,L,X,V,I), capitalized and interpreted as Roman numerals, have their values added up so as to give a hidden date. {see page 119 for example.]

H. Writing-paper quantities
   a. quire: 24 sheets
   b. ream: Formerly 20 quires; today, 500 sheets
   c. bundle: 1,000 sheets = 40 quires = 2 reams
   d. bale: 5,000 sheets, or 10 reams or 200 quires

I. Currency exchange, an immeasurably different experience: Become Worldly Wise by Exchanging Money: You've just inherited $100,000 from your favorite uncle. His bequest requires that you spend this money on travel to other countries. Plan a European trip by getting familiar with other countries' currencies and their exchange rates based on the United States Dollar (USD). Or, if you live in another country, learn its exchange rates with the countries to which you want to travel. How much money for each country do you plan to exchange?

   a. Get started by using the currency converter at:
http://finance.yahoo.com/currencyconverter?u#from=USD;to= EUR;amt=1

   b.   **Examples of other countries' moneys/currencies**
  1. England/Great Britain: **British pound** (GBP)
  2. African Countries:
     a. Algeria, Morocco and many other countries: **francs**
     b. Egypt: **pound**
     c. Ethiopia: **thalers**
     d. Ghana: **cedis**
     e. Kenya: **shillings**

   c.   **Teachers:**

  1. Encourage your students to create a journey that is possible by traveling through several adjacent countries.
  2. Or, help advanced students to create an imaginary country, then describe its location, climate, history, favorite sports, its currency, i.e.: I'm going to go to the island of Scara Dara for a year-long visit to help the natives _____.

http://www.maphistory.info/chronograms.html
http://www.easysurf.cc/menumt.htm
http://www.ex.ac.uk/cimt/dictunit/dictunit.htm
http://dmoz.org/Kids_and_Teens/School_Time/Science/Measurement/
http://www.nps.gov/whmi/educate/ortrtg/11or1.htm
http://www.vendian.org/mncharity/dir3/bodyruler_angle/
http://www.iofm.net/community/kidscorner/maths/origin.htm

   J.   **Modern-day Size/Length Measures:**

benchmark: A standard of comparison by which something can be measured or judged, a test, measure, mark, criterion, gauge, touchstone, yardstick, a surveyor's mark made on a stationary object of a previously determined position and elevation and used as a reference point in tidal observations and surveys.

em: A linear unit (1/6 inch) used in printing (from an original size of an "*M*.")

en: Half the width of an *em*

fathom: A unit of length equal to 6 feet (1.83 meters), originally, the space to which a man can extend his arms, used principally to measure the depth of navigable water by soundings.

furlong: A unit for measuring distance, particularly as lengths of horse races in the U. S., United Kingdom, and Ireland, equal to 1/8 mile (201 meters). Equal to 10 *chains* (*see* **Obsolete Measures** *below*). Furlong dates back at least to the ninth century and comes from the Old English words *furh* (furrow) and *lang* (long). It originally referred to the length of the furrow in one acre of a ploughed medieval communal field that was divided into strips.

hand: A unit of length equal to 4 inches (10.2 centimeters), used especially to specify the height of a horse. How many hands is the height of an average horse? Answer on page 233 of APPENDIX.

kiloton: A mass, 1000 tons (10,000 x 2000)

light-year: See above:

megaton: A million tons

micron: A unit of length equal to one millionth (10^{-6}) of a meter. It is no longer in technical use.

mil: A unit of length equal to one thousandth of an inch, used to specify thickness of sheets or wire

pica: A linear unit (1/6 inch) used in printing

score: A group of 20 items; a set of 20 members; A score of men were sent out, but only one returned. "Four score and seven years ago..." from Abraham Lincoln's Gettysburg Address. What is the next line in this speech? The normal lifespan in Biblical times was stated as 'three-score years and ten' (Psalm 90: 10). What would that normal age have been?

stone: A British measure of weight equal to 14 pounds/6.4 kilograms. Mr. Smith weighs 10 stones.

http://en.wikipedia.org/wiki/Hertz
http://www.techterms.com
http://www.practicalmoneyskills.com/english/index.php

Probe and Shed Light

K. File Size Units from Smallest to Largest

bit: The smallest unit in computing with a value of 1 or 0. You will probably not find a file size listed in bits. Think of this as a regular sized marble.

byte (pronounced "bite") is a unit of measurement of information storage, most often consisting of eight bits. Compared to a marble, this would be a baseball.

kilobyte (KB): A unit of approximately 1000 bytes (1024 to be exact). Most download sites use kilobytes when they give file sizes. A typical page of text is around 4KB.

megabyte (MB): A unit of approximately one million bytes (1,024 KB). Now for the leap— this would be a medium sized skyscraper. 1.44 Megabytes (1,474 KB) = 3.5" floppy disks; 650 Megabytes = 1 CD Rom or around 450 of those old 3.5 floppies.

giga: A system of units denoting 10^9, or 1,000,000,000 (1 thousand million)

gigabyte: Approximately 1 billion bytes (1024 MB); a unit of computer storage meaning either 1000^3 *bytes* or 1024^3 bytes (1000^3 = one billion). Take 1024 of medium-sized skyscrapers and stick them together for this one! Or one pick-up truck filled with books.

gigahertz: Used to measure computer processing speeds. At 2.45 gigahertz, a microwave oven operates at almost the same frequency as your computer's Wi-Fi connection.

gigaton: A metric unit of mass, equal to 1,000,000,000 (1 billion) metric tons, 1,000,000,000,000 (1 trillion) kilograms, or 1 quadrillion grams

petabyte: 1 million gigabytes + all material ever printed!

terabyte: 1,000,000,000,000 bytes, or 50,000 trees made into paper and printed + 1 TB

exabyte: 1,000,000,000,000,000,000 bytes—or all the words ever spoken by humans = 5EB

http://en.wikipedia.org/wiki/Hertz
http://www.techterms.com
http://www.practicalmoneyskills.com/english/index.php

L. Speeds: A mile a minute?

1. A **knot (kn)** is a unit of a boat's or an airplane's speed equal to one nautical mile per hour. 10 knots equals 11½ miles per hour.

2. An **anemometer,** a device attached to a weather vane, measures wind speed.

3. The Saffir-Simpson Hurricane Scale rates the wind intensity of **hurricane categories** at miles per hour (mph) and knots

   a. Category 1 winds: 74-95 mph/64-82 knots
   b. Category 2 winds: 96-110 mph/83-95 knots
   c. Category 3 winds: 111-130 mph/96-113 knots
   d. Category 4 winds: 131-155 mph/114-135 knots
   e. Category 5 winds: over 155 mph/135 knots

4. An **odometer** measures the speed at which a car is traveling.

5. **Light** travels at 186,282 miles per second! Or, stated in a more scientific way, light travels at 299,792,458 meters per second. How many miles does it travel in a minute? An hour? Answers in the Appendix on page 233

III. GRASP OUR GEOMETRIC WORLD

"Let us not go blindly through our beautiful world."
E.H.M.

A. Awaken Your Eyes To Your Environs

Get up close and personal for really good examinations. Take pictures of every sort of feature and shape. Put them together in a book—or make a poster.

Probe and Shed Light

1. Study construction cranes and scaffolding next to buildings. How many shapes do you see? If possible, walk around them and take pictures for later study.

2. Look at city buildings. Are their windows round? Diamond/ rhomboid? Square? What shape(s) are a variety of buildings' doors?

3. Find a water tower. If possible, park near by. Notice how its stuctuaral shapes change as you walk around it; how many can you find?

4. Take notice of buildings' roofs. There are only four basic styles. Can you sketch each? Name them? Hint: They are either gambrel, gable, mansard, or hip. (See hip roof and dormer windows on page 86.)

5. How many triangles can you find in a radio tower? Take a picture; count those you capture in your photo. Watch for similar pictures in your local newspaper.

6. Look for shrubs that have been trimmed to various shapes. In your neighborhood you will probably find at least one that has been clipped to a round shape. If you live where cacti grow, notice how different species have widely different shapes. If you don't have access to living cacti, go to http://www.cactus-succulents.com/cactus-photo-gallery.html. What shapes did you notice?

7. Hunt through magazines and newspapers for pictures of various shaped items. Look for lumber and other materials at building sites, geometric patterns on furniture, wallpaper designs, shapes of flooring tiles, window panes, chair backs, vehicles' steering wheels, fire hydrants, flower petals, fences, boats' sails, belt buckles, umbrellas, fruits, veggies, crackers, ice cream cones: In other words, look everywhere and at everything! Take pictures of these. Make a scrapbook or collage of your images.

B. Speak Graphically

1. Help children become facile with graphing by:
   a. Using data based on real life purchases at the grocery, the gas pump, and wherever you or they spend money.
   b. Studying local railroad or Amtrak schedules to compute times between several destinations and the cost of tickets for real or imaginary trips.
   c. Tracking your area's local races—running, horse, boating, swimming, etc.—to determine length and time of each lap.

2. Display Data With Diverse Ways

You can show information on many subjects, such as your money earned, test scores for different subjects, hours you worked and so forth by using pie charts, bar graphs, lines, and unusual shapes. Look at newspapers' graphic stock market information.

a. Become A Meteorologist: See page 208

b. Graph Diverse Information

1. **Line Graphs and Bar Charts** are among several ways to display facts and figures. Try them all. Decide a subject that you can use for each type of graph. Which do you think displays the information in the best manner? Use these sites for help:

http://nces.ed.gov/NCESKIDS/GRAPHING/classic/line.asp
http://www.superteacherworksheets.com/graphing.html

2. **Pie charts** are also ways to indicate various amounts. Go to the links below to see what they look like. What information do you have that you could show others with a pie chart?

http://en.wikipedia.org/wiki/Pie_chart
http://www.shodor.org/interactivate/activities/piechart/
http://nces.ed.gov/nceskids/createAgraph/

Here is a story to graph in any method you choose: On her first day at camp, Marsha caught two cod. On the second day she caught only one fish, but the third day was her lucky one—she caught three fish! You finish the tale: What did she catch on the fourth day? The fifth? The sixth? Now put this information on a graph. What was the average daily number of fish that Marsha caught?

Graph your favorite sports' teams' scores by the week and month. Other topics, real or imagined, you could graph: How many pushups did you do on each day of the week; the entire week? This month? Last month?

Create a graph showing how many miles Mario walked each day of one week to pick up trash along his town's roadways. Did he win a medal for collecting more than anyone else?

Other ways to find events or incidents (auto accidents; police arrests) to graph: Look through your local newspaper or USA Today°. If your family doesn't subscribe to either, go online for the latter's interesting graphs: http://www.usatoday.com/news/default.htm. Click on any of the papers' topics. "Money," is especially interesting; scroll down to its "Trackers and calculators" for several types of data.

3. **Pictograms** are like bar charts except they use a number of little pictures to show how many items there are in each row. You can be as creative as you want and have a great time showing data in an original form. Your computer, or one at a nearby library or university, will have picture fonts. The one below is *Wingdings*°. Other picture fonts are *Webdings*°, *Dingbats*°

Number of males who earned more than $50,000,000:

http://gwydir.demon.co.uk/jo/numbers/pictogram/info.htm

For more ideas and help, go to: http://www.coolmath.com/graphit/

3. **Amuse Yourself With Math**

   a. **Work a Sudoku*** a day to keep the brain awake!

   http://www.sudoku.com/justforkids.html
   http://www.websudoku.com/ebook.php?ll

   b. **Solve Cryptograms***: Encoded messages, whereby each letter in the message is replaced with a different **letter of the alphabet.** Every time a particular letter occurs in the message, it is replaced with the **same** code letter. To solve a cryptogram, look for the most frequently used letters (often vowels, "t", and "s" and clues the show letter patterns.

   UXBH MCYH XJ KPO YCTR CU, DOU RPT'U MHXEII CU UVXU ZXK. Hints: What word often follows a comma? What word often uses an apostrophe? Think of 4-letter words that start and end with the same letter. (Answer in Appendix page 233) Go to http://www.cryptograms.org/ for more of these puzzles.

   c. **Play Kakuro,*** (also called **cross sums**) a game similar to crossword puzzles and cryptograms. These logic puzzles are basically crosswords in which digits from 1 through 9 are entered into the spaces of the diagram instead of letters. To learn more, go to http://en.wikipedia. org/wiki/Kakuro, and www.dellmagazines.com/samplepuzzles/ KakuroSamplePuzzle and www.kakuropuzzle.com/.

*You will find these and other puzzles online or in puzzle magazines sold in newsstands, bookstores, grocery stores, etc.

MORE RESOURCES:

http://www.puzzability.com/sampler/index.html
http://www.learner.org/interactives/dailymath/resources.html
http://www.dmoz.org/Kids_and_Teens/School_Time/Math/Math_for_Fun/
http://www.mathpuzzle.com/27Oct05.html
http://www.mste.uiuc.edu/courses/ci336kt/kauwell/edisonlinks.htm

Math Puzzles & Oddities by R.A. Yawin: Games, Gamebooks, Crosswords
http://www.antiqbook.com/boox/top/315922.shtml
Magic House of Numbers. Irving Adler: http://www.ecrater.com/product.
php?pid=3116787
Math Site for Kids and Teens: http://www.edinformatics.com/kids_teens/kt_
math.htm
Math in daily life with math interactives: Geometry 3D shapes, math in daily
life, metric conversions, statistics:
The triangle arithmetics by Leo Brueckner: https://www.alibris.com/search/
books/author/Brueckner,%20Leo%20J

C. **Increase Your Mathematical Wisdom: Think In Terms Of Today's Billions—Or Beyond!**

1.   If you have trouble picturing today's news and the differences between millions, billions and trillions, get these:

        a.   A person who is a million seconds old is 12 days old.

        b.   A person who is a billion seconds is 31 years old.

        c.   A person who is a trillion seconds old was a Neanderthal—that was 31,688 years ago.

        d.   A million minutes ago was just about one year ago. A billion minutes ago was the year A.D. 1.

        e.   So what could you do with an AIG bonus of $165 million? If you make $40,000 a year, you'd have to work 4,125 years to earn $165 million.

                1.   You could buy top-of-the-line BMWs for 2,062 friends.

                2.   You could buy a $452,000 home every day for a year.

                3.   You could cover 42 football fields with $10 bills.

        f.   What could you buy with a $183 billion? For an example, read what the CIA World Factbook states: Uruguay's gross domestic product—all goods and services produced in the country—at $42.7 billion for 2008. The factbook puts the GDP (Gross Domestic Product) of the Bahamas at $9.2 billion last year. Cambodia's GDP was $29.2 billion ... Together, that brings you up to only $81.1 billion.

g. So, if you happened to have $183 billion, what countries would **you** buy? $183 billion is certainly a huge measure, almost beyond our abilities to understand, but it's not as scary as an even larger mind-blowing term: An **exabyte**! Think about this: "5 exabytes equal **all the words ever spoken by human beings!**"

Exabyte (derived from the SI prefix *exa-*) is a unit of information or computer storage equal to one quintillion bytes. It is commonly abbreviated **EB**. When used with byte multiples, the SI prefix may indicate a power of either 1000 or 1024, so the exact number may be either: 1,000,000,000,000,000,000 bytes 1000^6, or 10^{18}; or 1,152,921,504,606,846,976 bytes—1024^6, or 2^{60}.

http://en.wikipedia.org/wiki/Exabyte
http://www.theeldergeek.com/bits_to_exabytes_-_size_relationships.html.

D. FUN AND GAMES

1. Roman Numerals

a. **Add Roman Numerals** left to right: MCCLXI = 1,000 + 200 + 50 + 10 + 1 = 1,261. If the numeral on the right is larger than the one on its left, subtract the smaller number from the larger. Add each result. MCMXLII = 1000 + 900 + 40 + 2 = 1,942.

b. Make flash cards for first-time learners or for a refresher course:

I, II, III, IV, V, VI, VII, VIII, IX, X, XI, XII, XIII, XIV, XV, XVI, XVII, XVIII, XVIV, XV, XVI, XVII, XVIII, XX, XXI, etc., **XXX, XL, LX LXX, LXXX, XC, CI, CII**, etc., **CXX, CXXX, CXL, CL ... CC**; ... **CD** (400); ...**D** (500)**; DC; DCC; DCCC; CM**; **M** (1000); **MDC** (1600); **MDCC** (1700); **MCM** 1900); **MM** (2000).

Probe and Shed Light

   c. Practice
1. Write your birth year in Roman Numerals.
2. A statue in Rome has this date on it: CDV. What year does this represent? (405)
3. A stone in my town has this date on it: MCMIII. What year was that? (1903)
4. Put these Roman Numerals fractions into their lowest form.

    (a) $\dfrac{III}{IX}$ =___   (b) $\dfrac{V}{X}$ =___   (c) $\dfrac{X}{XII}$ =___

    (d) $\dfrac{L}{C}$ =___   (e) $\dfrac{XC}{C}$ =___

(Answers: (1) 3/9 = 1/3; (2) 5/19 = ½; (3) 10/12 = 5/6; (4) 50/100 = ½; (5) 90/100 = 8/10)

5. Find more Roman numeral words: DIM, MILD, CIVIL CIVIC, LIVID, MIMIC, VIVID, I'LL, DILL, MIX, LID, MILL...

2. **Chronograms*** (Greek *chronos* ("time") + *gramma* ("letter") = time writing. Sentences or inscriptions in which Roman numbers, when added together, stand for a particular date. (U's stand for V's.)

   a. **Example** 1: **M**y **D**ay **I**s **C**losed **I**n **I**mmortality = 1000 + 500 + 1 + 100 + 1 + 1 + 1603. This chronogram was written to commemorate the death of Queen Elizabeth I of England. The capitalized letters (MDICII) represent the year of Elizabeth's death.
   b. **C**o**V**rteo**V**s reader, **I** finish with this **C**hronogra**M**. Be the year **It** **I**n**V**o**LV**es happy to **V**s both. farewe**LL**.
   c. C + V + V + I + C + M + I + I + V + L + V + V + L + L. 100 + 5 + 5 + 1 + 100 + 1000 + 1 + 1 + 5 + 50 + 5 + 5 + 50 + 50 = 1872

3. **Mathematical Progressions:** What comes next? Answers in Appendix, page 14

a. 1 3 5 7 __ __ __ __

b. A26 B25 C24 ____ ____ ____

c. 2 4 2 8 2 16 __ __ __

d. ZA YB XC ____ ____ ____

e. 5 6 8 11 15 __ __ __

f. A B D G K __ __ __

g. 1/2 1/4 1/6 1/8 ____ ____ ____

h. A N B O C P ____ ____ ____

i. 3 7 15 31 ____ ____

j. BOY THREE CROWD FIVE JAM _____

k. 3600 1800 600 150 (30 ... 5)

l. 1   2   3   5   8   13   21: ___   ___   ___
(1 + 2 = 3; 2 + 3 = 5; 3 + 5 = 8; 5 + 8 = 13; 6 + 13 = 21)

m. 1940 (plus4); 1944 (plus 8); 1952; 1964; 1980   ?

4. **Alphametics/Cryptarithms Examples and Rules*:** The same letter always stands for the same digit, which is always represented by the same letter. The letter **O** always stands for 0. There cannot be a leading "**O**."

a. B O Y
    X   25
    ARBO

b. S E N D
    M O R E
    MONEY

c.   WRONG
    + WRONG
       RIGHT

Two wrongs do make a right!

d.
```
                    HOE
         HEN │ LOVES
                    I L L
                    I OE
                    HEN
                    HNIS
                    HHLS
                    RS
```
Answers in Appendix Page 233

5. **Reduce fractions to lowest common denominator**. Rules from 2 to 10 for Grades 6-8:

   a. A number is divisible by:

   2 if it ends in an even number such as 977558, it is divisible by 2 because 8 is an even number.

   3 If the sum of the number's digits is divisible by three, then the number is also divisible by three. (i.e. 163, 279, 597)

   4 If the number formed by its last two digits is divisible by 4, the original number is also, so 17327829892648648264421834612 is divisible by 4 because 12 is divisible by 4.

   5 If the number ends in 5 or 0

   6 If it is an even number and is divisible by 3

   7 If the last digit is doubled and subtracted from the other digit(s) and the resulting number is divisible by 7, then the whole number is also divisible by 7; i.e. 182 (subtract 2 x 2 from 18; the resulting 14 is divisible by 7), 483 (subtract 3 x 2 from 48; the resulting 42 is divisible by 7); if the number is very large, repeat the process until you reach a number you know is divisible by 7

   8 If the last three digits of a number are divisible by 8, then so is the whole number. 32176888 is divisible by 8 but 3217886 isn't

9 If the sum of its digits is divisible by 3 or 9, it is divisible by 9; i.e. 1467, 972

10 If the number ends in 0.

6. **Apply Divisibility Rules** for reducing fractions to lowest numbers: (Grades 6-8). Write these numbers on individual cards; **students determine their divisibility by 2, 3, 4, 5, 6, 7, 8, 9, 10 or prime**:

351	25	293	474	69
91	496	110	340	145
181	130	133	161	89
753	265	295	858	272
171	78	203	790	136
68	81	367	117	246
183	411			

a. **Answers** (in ranking order):
    25: 5; **68**: 2, 4; **69**: 3; **78**: 2, 3, 6; **81**: 3, 9; **89 prime; 91**: 7; **110**: 2, 5, 10; **117**: 3,9; **130**: 2, 5, 10; **133**: 7; **136**: 2, 3; **145**: 5; **161**: 7; **171**: 3, 9; **181 prime; 183**: 3; **203 prime; 246**: 2, 3, 6; **265**:5; **272**: 2, 4; **293 prime; 295** 5; **340**: 2, 4, 5, 10; **351**: 3; **367 prime; 411**: 3; **474**: 2, 3, 6; **496**: 2,4; **753**: 3; **790**: 2, 5, 10; **858**: 2, 3, 6

b. **Prime numbers are** those that are **divisible only by 1 and themselves**. The following numbers up to 300 are prime:
    2, 3, 5, 7, 11, 13, 17, 19, 23, 29, 31, 37, 41, 43, 47, 53, 59, 61, 67, 71, 73, 79, 83, 89, 97, 101, 103, 107, 109, 113, 127, 131, 137, 139, 149, 151, 157, 163 167, 173,179, 181, 191, 193, 197, 199, 211, 223, 227, 229, 233, 239, 241, 251, 257, 263, 269, 271, 277, 281, 283 and 293

7. **Play Math Master, a group game.** Give each student a typed sheet of several rows (one for each game) of numbers from 1 through 100. Students mark out numbers based on the clues given by the Math Master.

Probe and Shed Light

a. **I'm thinking of a number:**

1. It is divisible by 3, 5, 9. What is it?
2. It is divisible by 3, 7, 9.
3. It is divisible by 2, 3, 4, 6, 7
4. It is divisible by 2, 3, 4, 5, 6, 10
5. It is divisible by 2, 3, 4, 6, 8, 9

(Answer in Appendix, page 233)

b. **I'm thinking of another number:**

1. It is greater than 50
2. Not divisible by 2
3. Not divisible by 5
4. Nor 7
5. Nor 9
6. It is not a prime number.
7. Only 5 numbers are left (51, 57, 69, 87, 93). It is the one whose digits have a sum different than the sums of the other digits. (Answer in Appendix, page 233)

c. **I'm thinking of another number:**

1. It is not a multiple of 12
2. It is greater than the number of inches in 2 yards + 10 inches
3. It is less than 5 score
4. It is not divisible by 5
5. It is not divisible by 2
6. It is not a prime number.
   This leaves 3 digits (87, 93, 99). The one I'm thinking of has the lowest sum of the digits. (Answer in Appendix, page 233)

8. **Check your work by casting out nines:** Make sure answers to addition, subtraction, multiplication, and division problems are correct in the easiest, fastest and most reliable way. It will be all students' joy! Guaranteed! You'll have to do it several times before you "see" how it works.

Let's start with an addition problem:
$$\begin{array}{r} \mathbf{4763} \\ \underline{\mathbf{3275}} \\ \mathbf{8038} \end{array}$$

Add the numbers in the **sum**, casting out/deleting sums of 9:
Top row: $(4 + 7 = 11 - 9 = 2)$; $(2 + 6 = 8)$ $(8 + 3 = 11)$; $(11 - 9 = 2)$;
Second row: $(3 + 2 = 5 + 7 + 12 - 9 = 3 + 5 = \mathbf{8}$
Add sums of these rows: $2 + 8 - 9 = 1$
Answer row: $(8 + 0 + 3 = 11 - 9 = 2 + 8 = 10 - 9 = \mathbf{1}$, thus verifying that 8038 is correct.
Now practice with this addition; is the sum correct? Yes/No? How do you know?

$$\begin{array}{rl} 8625 & 3 \\ \underline{3964} & \underline{4} \\ 12589 & 7 \end{array}$$

Use the same method for subtracting and multiplying.

Good explanations are at: http://www.themathlab.com/natural/mental%20 math%20tricks/casting%20nines/casting.htm

9. The **Trachtenberg** speed system of multiplying by 11 or 12 will please mathematically inclined students. It's actually quite fun and not very hard. Students just have to learn the rules and perform a little practice!

   a. **To multiply by 11:**

      1. Put down the right-hand number of the multiplicand (the number to be multiplied) as the right-hand number of the answer;

      2. To get the succeeding numbers, simply add each number to its neighbor at the right;

      3. The left-hand number of the multiplicand becomes the left-hand number of the answer.

Example: 623 x 11 = <u>623 x 11</u> ; <u>623 x 11</u> ; <u>623 x 11</u> ; <u>623 x 11</u>
                              3   53   853   6853

(Use a dot above and to the left of the number to show a carry.)

b. **To multiply by 12:**

    1. Double the right-hand number of the multiplicand and put it down as the right-hand number of the answer;

    2. Double each succeeding number and add to its neighbor at the right;

    3. The left-hand number of the multiplicand (plus anything you carry) becomes the left-hand number of the answer.

Example: 564 x 12 = <u>564 x12</u> ; <u>564 x12</u> ; <u>564 x12</u> ; <u>564 x12</u>
                              8   68   768   6768

http://www.themathlab.com/natural/mental%20math%20tricks/casting%20nines/casting.htm
http://wildaboutmath.com/2008/02/15/trachtenberg-speed-multiplication-exploring-why-it-works/
http://geniuswriter.sulekha.com/blog/post/2007/02/trachtenberg-speed-system-of-basic-mathematics.htm

10. Mental division short-cuts

    a. To divide by 25, multiply by 4 and divide by 100.
    b. To divide by 50 multiply by 2 and divide by 100.
    c. To divide by 12 ½, multiply by 8 and divide by 100.
    d. To divide by 33 1/3, multiply by 3 and divide by 100.
    e. To divide by 125, multiply by 8 and divide by 1000.
    f. To find short cuts for dividing numbers by 7, 11, or 13, go to: http://www.murderousmaths.co.uk/BOOKS/BKMM1x11.htm

11. Sports Math[*]

> *If I were to say, "God, why me?" about the bad things,*
> *then I should have said, "God, why me?*
> **Arthur Ashe**

One way to make mathematics exciting—to say nothing of relevant—for many students is to provide a teacher/school-generated activity that I call Sports Math®. Each unit uses estimating, adding, subtracting, map work, understanding team names, etc., regardless of the sport. In many situations, students will see how addition and multiplication are the same. Some activities involve using parentheses and even brackets and require critical thinking as scores increase.

Although I did not devise this unit to make students fans of any particular sport, it provides an awareness and understanding of games along with their local, national, and international ranges. Correlate math instruction in gym classes by having students measure the playing areas of the game(s) they choose.

Each year teach the Sports Math® unit at different seasons of the year, so that football, for instance, would be the sport of study only once every four years or so, with baseball, basketball, soccer, or other sports in turn. Although the unit can apply to national teams, it may be even more interesting to follow local boys' and girls' high school teams.

a. For **football**, students must know:

1 point: extra point after a touchdown
2 points: safety
3 points: field goal
6 points: touchdown

b. For **baseball**, assign reluctant readers to give reports on various players' biographies. All can measure distances on the field and write letters to team members or team owners, requesting the latter for decals.

Encourage more advanced students to find ways to restate some of the possible scores, i.e. if the team's score was 8 points, it could have been derived from a touchdown and a touch back (6 + 2), four touch backs (as unlikely as they may be in the real game), which can be expressed arithmetically as 2 + 2 + 2 + 2 or 4 x 2 or even (2 + 2) x 2, and two field goals and a touch back, 3 + 3 + 2 or (2 x 3) + 2.

Probe and Shed Light

Can your students explain the various ways a football team could achieve the scores below.

1. 5 points? 3 + 2 = A field goal and a safety

2. 6 points? 2 field goals = 3 + 3; or 3 safeties = 2 + 2 + 2; or touchdown and missed extra point

3. 7 points? 6 + 1; or [3 + (2 x 2)]

4. 8 points? (6 + 2; 2 + 2 + 2 + 2, 4 x 2; 3 + 3 + 2): touchdown + 2 point conversion

5. 9 points? (6 + 1 + 2; 3 + 3 + 3; 2 + 2+ 2 + 3)

6. 10 points? (6 + 1 +3; 6 + 2 + 2; 2 + 2 + 3 + 3)

Ask students to make up their own score and call on classmates to decide all the possible ways it could be achieved. Or, ask students to discover a score that was made in the following way: 1 touchdown, 1 extra point, 1 field goal; etc.

c. **Basketball** is particularly easy for gathering information about both boy and girl players. What are the average heights of a boys' or girls' team? Also, typical scores in basketball provide more difficult arithmetic than those of football. **Volleyball** is another good sport to follow. Perhaps a group of students could go together to attend local basketball or volleyball games—and do the math.

Brainstorming with others will lead to many ways to use Sports Math˙, and students will learn about competing teams.

10. Math Bingo

This game reinforces basic addition, subtraction, multiplication, and division facts and allows for exercises in mental math and prime numbers. Each student has a bingo card on which are whole numbers, fractions, percents, and Roman numerals as answers to problems either held up by the emcee for ten seconds on large cards that are easily visible to all students or displayed on an overhead projector.

Students must work quickly to solve the problems (see examples below), covering the space on their cards with squares of cardboards if the problem's answer appears there. You can make game cards to reinforce skills at all levels of third grade and above. The B column holds answers from 0 19; **I**: 20-39, **N**: 40-59; **G**: 60-79; **O**: 80-99. Be sure to have a few small prizes to give to winners! There are many websites that offer bingo for teachers.

a. **Number of Players**: Whole group of similar abilities

b. **Time To Play:** 40 - 55 minutes

c. **Materials**: Overhead projector for transparencies with math problems or blackboard, Bingo cards, and Bingo "chips"

d. **Rules**: This game is played with regular Bingo cards, which use the numbers 1 - 99. Instead of calling out "B-9," project a math problem that has the answer 9 onto the screen, or write it on the board. For example, find the cost of renting a saw for 2 hours if it rents for $4.50 per hour. The math problems are uncovered one at a time. Students solve the problems and then mark the cards.

e. **Winning the Game**: A student with five in a row under one of the BINGO letters calls out "Bingo!" The teacher confirms the winning card. The game continues until the prize(s) are distributed. The person who wins the first Bingo is eligible to win a second Bingo on the same card.

f. **Management**:

1. Allow students to work together in teams of two or three. This helps the review process. Give hints to the class when needed.

Probe and Shed Light

2. About 10 minutes before the end of the period, just turn off the projector or erase the board and call out the numbers until the classroom has a winner.

3. **Create Bingo Cards**

B: Answers must be between 0 – 19: 8 x 2; 25-18; 8/12 + 1/3; 11- 5 1/2; 50% of 24

I: Answers must be between 20-39: 40-19; 8x5- 5; XXXVI; 9x3

N. Answers must be between 40-59: 70-15; next prime after 31; 7 x 7; 20% of 250; 27 + 32

G. Answers must be between 60-79: 64 + 12; 9 x 7; 100-31; 8 x 9

O. Answers must be between 80-99: (9 x 8) + 12; XCVII; 100-9; 200-103

4. **Sample Card**

B	I	N	G	O
3/4	2	55	72	91
5	21	49	63	84
0	35	FREE	60	94
5 ½	25%	50	76	97
8	36	37	69	82

There are many Internet sites with examples and downloadable files for BINGO

11. Play Math Games With Cards!

Strengthen your students' knowledge of arithmetical facts and test their mental agility with numbers by using playing cards on which you apply your numbers over the original cards' values. As children enjoy these games, they gain mastery of important facts!

To customize a deck of regular playing cards, buy small-size labels at any office supply store. Put two of the same number on each card: One at the top left corner, the other, upside down, on the opposite corner, so no matter which way the cards are turned, students can read them easily. Be sure that each deck has four cards of the same value. You will need anywhere from 24 cards for some sets up to a full deck (52) for others. Ask friends for their extra decks. The numbers below represent a set geared for the second half of first grade or higher, according to your group's general abilities. Only you can decide which sets meet the needs of your children.

6 – 1	5 + 3	4 + 3	3 + 3	2 + 7	2 + 8
1 + 8	3 + 6	4 + 6	3 + 7	8 + 2	4 + 1
2 + 3	7 – 1	5 + 2	4 + 4	2 + 6	3 + 2
5 + 4	4 + 2	9 – 1	3 + 4	2 + 4	2 + 5

How to Play: Once the cards have their numeric values, children can play Go Fish or Concentration/Memory.

1. **GO FISH!** Best for 3-4 players but 2 may also play. Using a standard 52-card deck, the dealer deals 5 cards to each player (7 each for 2 players). He places the remaining cards face down to form a stock. The player to dealer's left starts the play by asking another player for a specific mathematical equivalent.

Probe and Shed Light

For example, if it is my turn, I might say: "'Mary, please give me your fives." I must already hold at least one card whose value is equivalent to five. If the player who was asked (Mary) has cards of the named rank (fives in this case), she must give all her cards of this rank to me. Then I get another turn and may again ask any player for any rank that I hold.

If Mary does not have any cards of the named rank, she says, "Go fish!" I then draw the top card from the stock. If I draw a card of the rank I asked for, I show it and get to draw another card from the stock. If the card I draw is not the rank I asked for, I keep it, but the turn now passes to the next player to my left.

As soon as a player collects a book of 4 cards of the same rank, he must show it and place it face down in front of him. The game continues until either someone has no cards left in his hand or the stock runs out. The winner is the player who has the most books.

2. **CONCENTRATION** aka **MEMORY** is a game requiring a good memory, an occasional lucky guess, and the matching of mathematical equivalents. Thoroughly shuffle decks of cards containing 20, 24, 28 or 32 cards conforming to the grade that will be playing, then lay all the cards face down on the playing surface. Whoever is to the left of the dealer begins the play by selecting any two cards from the array. He must turn each card over, lay it down flat so that other players see it, and state the value of each. Others in the game should be alert to speak up in case the player makes a mistake.

The object for each player is to match the mathematical equivalent of one card to the same mathematical equivalent of another. If the player does not have a match, he turns the cards back face down **in the same location**, and the next player takes a turn. The locations of the cards must never change during a game. When a player makes a match, he keeps the pair in front of him and takes another turn. The player with the greatest number of pairs is the winner.

Grade 1: beginner —20 cards

1 + 2	2 + 1	0 + 3	4 - 1	0 + 4	1 + 3
1 + 5	3 + 3	4 + 2	7 - 1	0 + 7	1 + 6
2 + 2	5 - 1	1 + 4	3 + 2	4 + 1	6 – 1
2 + 5	8 – 1				

Grade 1— 32 cards

6 -1	15 + 3	4 + 3	1 + 3	2 + 2	2 + 8
1 + 8	3 + 6	4 + 6	3 + 7	8 + 2	4 + 1
2 + 3	7 - 1	3 + 1	4 + 4	2 + 6	3 + 2
5 + 4	4 + 2	3 + 3	3 + 4	2 + 4	2 + 5
5 + 2	7 + 2	5 - 1	9 - 1	3 + 0	2 + 1
4 - 1	5 – 2				

Grade 2: 20 cards

5 + 9	6 + 8	15 - 3	8 + 6	5 + 7	8 + 4
13 - 2	3 + 8	8 + 5	15 - 5	9 + 4	10 + 3
6 + 7	5 + 6	15 - 4	7 + 3	19 - 9	7 + 7
12 - 2	9 + 3				

Grade 3A: 24 cards

4 + 3	12- 2	20 - 10	5 + 6	9 - 2	8 - 2
5 + 1	6 + 3	10 - 4	11 - 2	12 – 3	4 + 2
3 + 8	5 + 2	10 - 2	5 + 3	12 – 4	15 - 4
6 + 2	4 + 7	7 + 3	10 - 3	5 + 4	4 + 6

Grade 3B: 24 cards

9 + 7	6 + 7	15 - 2	5 + 8	10 + 4	8 + 6
12 + 3	4 + 8	28 - 12	6 + 8	7 + 8	15 - 3
7 + 5	20 - 2	9 + 9	3 + 9	10 + 8	12 + 6
18 -- 2	4 + 9	6 + 9	10 + 5	7 + 7	11 + 5

Grade 4: 30 cards

XXX	45 - 15	42 - 12	21 + 9	11+ 16	35 - 8
18 + 9	21 + 6	XXV	16 + 9	18 + 7	36- 1
XX	32 - 12	12 + 8	4 x 5	XII	20 - 8
19 - 7	4 x 3	XVIII	3 x 6	35-20	5 x 3
XV	9 + 6	30 - 12			

Grade 5a: Reduce to lowest denominator (24 cards)

8 / 12	18 / 27	14 / 21	10 / 15	2 / 8	5 / 20
4 / 16	7 / 28	8 / 48	6 / 36	4 / 24	2 / 12
3 / 9	5 / 15	2 / 6	8 / 24	2 / 10	4 / 20
6 / 30	8 / 40	5 / 10	3 / 6	14 / 28	18 / 36

Grade 5b (24 cards)

L	43 + 7	30 + 20	38 + 7	9 x 5	52 - 7
30 + 12	50 – 8	38 + 12	XL	34 + 6	XLV
XLII	8 x 5	55 – 15	XXXV	29 + 6	41 – 6
27 + 8	25 + 8	20 + 13	6 x 7	11 x 3	XXXIII

Grades 6-8 (28 cards) Reduce to lowest common denominator

40 / 64	30 / 48	28 / 32	42 / 48	10 / 16	6 / 8
20 / 32	12 / 20	6 / 10	8 / 64	4 / 32	24 /32
12 / 16	24 /40	20 /24	30 / 36	18 / 30	14 /16
56 / 64	6 / 16	6 / 48	40 /48	12 / 32	10 /12
15 / 20	24 / 64	9 /12	2 / 16		

Grades 6-8 (28 cards): Reduce to lowest common denominator

60 %	.6	3/5	9 / 15	66 2/3 %	.66 2/3
2/3	10/15	75 %	.75	3/4	24 / 32
80 %	.8	4/5	20 / 25	37 1/2 %	.37 1/2
3/8	9/24	62 1/2 %	.62 1/2	5/8	10/16
87 1/2 %	87 1/2	7/8	14/16		

Grades 6-8 (24 cards)

XLVIII	37 + 11	60 – 12	(100 / 2) - 2	XLII
LII	40 + 12	28 + 14	60 - 18	(100/2) + 2
XLV	(80/2) + 5	64 – 19	33 + 12	XXX1X
21 x 2	60 - 12	23 + 16	(80 / 2) - 1	50 - 11
XXXIII	57 - 24	66 / 2	19 + 14	

MATH REFERENCES: Try them all!
For more mathematical activities, go to: http://homeschoolmath.blogspot.com/
Higher-thinking Math Tasks: Mathematical Mystery Tour by Mark Wahl.
http://www.markwahl.com/mathematical_mystery_tour.htm
http://www.mcs.surrey.ac.uk/Personal/R.Knott/Fibonacci/

The Joy of Mathematics on 2 CDs from The Teaching Company for older or advanced students: http://www.teach12.com, plus other mathematics courses
http://www.wieser-ed.com/previews/MM7371/: AGS consumer mathematics; high interest instructional materials for struggling learners
Consumer Mathematics In Christian Perspective by Judy Howe
http://www.aimsedu.org/.webloc
http://www.amazon.ca/ (fraction #6EA65)
http://www.amazon.com/Math

http://www.amazon.com/Piece-Wit-sharpening-Brain-bruising-Number-crunchingActivities/dp/1593631200
http://www.auntymath.com/
http://caca.essortment.com/teachingchildre_rbyv.htm
http://www.christianbook.com/html/specialty/1016.html?p=1018818
http://homeschooling.gomilpitas.com/explore/math.htm
http://homeschoolshopr.proboards37.com/index
http://www.iofm.net/community/kidscorner/maths/origin.htm
http://mathforum.org/
http://mathforum.org/t2t/thread.taco?thread=1726
http://www.bagatrix.com/prealgebra.htm
http://www.bridge.net/~labush/lalmwk6.htm: info & quiz on amounts of coins
http://www.coolmath.com/
http://www.ed.gov/pubs/parents/Math/index.html
http://www.edu.gov.on.ca/eng/document/brochure/earlymath/
http://www.Everydayspacesinc.com/
http://homeschooling.gomilpitas.com/materials/Materials.htm
http://shopping.msn.com/prices/shp/?itemId=492669141: The New Totally Awesome Money Book for Kids (and Their Parents)
http://www.k12.wa.us/CurriculumInstruct/mathematics/pubdocs/pdf/math.pdf
http://www.math.com/parents/articles/funmath.html
http://www.mathgoodies.com/
http://www.mrsvandyke.com/mathsites.htm
http://www.nhen.org/nhen/pov/editors/default.asp?id=110
http://www.nncc.org/Curriculum/sac52_math.science.girls.html
http://www.shodor.org/interactivate/
http://www.time4learning.com/fourth-grade-math.shtml

MATH CLUBS:

http://www.girlsangle.org/
http://www.mathpentath.org/gettingstarted/mathclubs.html
http://www.uwlax.edu/Mathematics/dept/Activities/Math%20Club.htm
http://www.math.uncc.edu/~hbreiter/clubs/mmc.htm
http://www.txstate.edu/mathworks/teacher/kidsmath/clubsuggestions.html
http://mathforum.org/t2t/thread.taco?thread=1726
http://www.uwlax.edu/Mathematics/dept/Activities/Math%20Club/Math%20Club.htm

THESE SELECTED TITLES SHOULD MEASURE UP! Available through AIMS: Association of Independent Maryland Schools and perhaps online. Created by Mary L. Williams Curriculum Materials Library Staff, 001 Willard Hall, Oklahoma State University, Stillwater, OK 74078

Alexander, Ruth Bell <u>Fraction Jugglers: A Math Gamebook for Kids + Their Parents</u>.

Ameis, Jerry <u>Mathematics on the Internet: A Resource for K-12 Teachers</u>.

Barbarash, Lorraine <u>Multicultural Games</u>. 1997

Benedick, Jeanne <u>Markets: From Barter to Bar Codes</u>. 1997

Berg, Adrianne G. <u>The Totally Awesome Money Book for Kids and Their Parents</u>.

Bokhari, Naila. <u>Piece of Pi: Wit - sharpening, Brain - Busting, Number - Crunching Activities with Pi</u>

Braddon, Kathryn. <u>Math Through Children's Literature</u>.

Bryant-More, Karen. <u>Usborne Math Skills-Adding and Subtracting Puzzles.</u>; <u>Multiplying and Dividing Puzzles.</u>

Callard-Szulgit, Rosemary. <u>Mind-Bending Math and Science Activities for Gifted Students (K-12)</u>

Clark, Dave. <u>More Tic-Tac-Toe Math</u>.

Coates, Grace Davila. <u>Family Math 2</u>.

Cook, Allen. <u>Content Area Mathematics for Secondary Teachers: The Problem Solver. Computer</u>

Confor, Chris. <u>Math by all Means: Geometry, Grade 2</u>.

Echols, Jean. <u>Ant Homes Under the Ground</u>

Egan, Lorraine Hopping. <u>25 Super Cool Math Board Games</u>

Eichinger, John. <u>40 Strategies for Integrating Science and Mathematics Instruction</u>

Forsten, Char. <u>Teaching Thinking and Problem Solving in Math</u>

Gossett, Carol and Evalyn Hoover. <u>Winter Wonders: Activities Integrating Math and Science</u>

Guthrie, Donna <u>Real World Math: Money and Other Numbers in Your Life</u>.

Hemmerich, Hal <u>Primetime: Strategies for Lifelong Learning in Mathematics and Science in the Middle and High School Grades</u>

Hewitt, Sally:<u>Timing</u>

Hightower, Susan <u>Twelve Snails to One Lizard: A Tale of Mischief and Measurement</u>

-----. <u>Numbers</u>

-----. <u>Puzzles</u>

-----. Shapes

-----. Sorting and Sets

Hume, Barbara Math on Display: Creative Activities for Teaching Math to Children Aged 5-8

Jenkins, Robert Cooperative Learning Activities in Algebra I

Kaye, Peggy Games for Math: Playful Ways to Help Your Child Learn Math

Keller, Elle. Animal Math

Kellison, Catherine The Playground of Mathematics

Kluger-Bell, Barry The Exploratorium Guide to Scale and Structure: Activities for the Elementary Classroom.

Kohl, Maryann MathArts: Exploring Math Through Art for 3 to 6 Year-Olds

Kopp, Jaine Early Adventures in Algebra

-----. Frog Math: Predict, Ponder, Play

-----. The Rainbow Mathematics

-----. Treasure Boxes

Krulik, Stephen Teaching Middle School Mathematics Activities, Materials, and Problems

Kuhs, Measure for Measure Using Portfolios in K-8 Math

Lobosco, Michael Mental Math Workout

McMillan, Bruce Jelly Beans for Sale

Martinez, Joseph G. R. Reading and Writing to Learn Mathematics

Marsh, Valerie Story Puzzles: Tales in the Tangram Tradition

Markle, Sandra. Measuring Up!: Experiments, Puzzles and Games Exploring Measurement.

McLoughlin, John Grant Calendar Problems

Muschla, Judith Algebra Teacher's Activities Kit

Posamentier, Alfred S. 101+ Great Ideas for Introducing Key Concepts in Mathematics: A Resource for Secondary School Teachers

Schiller, Pam. Count on Math: Activities for Small Hands and Lively Minds

Sharman, Lydia The Amazing Book of Shapes: Explore Math Through Shapes and Patterns

Sohns, Marvin L The Measurement Book

Tucker, Benny F. Teaching Mathematics to All Children: Designing and Adapting Instruction to Meet the Needs of Diverse Learners

Welchman-Tischler, Rosamond. How to Use Children's Literature To Teach Mathematics.

What's Math Got to Do with It? Level 2.

Wheatly, Grayson H. <u>Coming to Know Numbers: A Mathematical Activity Resource for Elementary School</u>; <u>Developing Mathematical Fluency: Activities for Grades 5 – 8</u>

<u>Math Games and Activities</u>; <u>More Math Games and Activities</u>; <u>The Multicultural Math Classroom</u>

CHAPTER VII

▼

FAMILY HOME WORK

Many family activities come to my mind, but since families can differ in a variety of ways, I provide a few I believe that fit all. Whether families homeschool their children or not, they have their own values, beliefs, and interests. I hope my readers will find many of my ideas to be useful and fun.

A. **Memory Gems For Family Fun** add to cultural literacy, improve memorization skills, provide worthwhile concepts, and open doors for family discussions.

1. If a task is once begun
    Never leave it till it's done;
    Be the labor great or small
    Do it well, or not at all. **Phoebe Cary**

2. Praise God for wheat, so white and sweet,
    Of which we make out bread!
    Praise God for yellow corn, with which
    His waiting world is fed! **Edward Everett Hale**

3. One rule to guide us in our life
    Is always good and true;
    'Tis, do to others as you would
    That they should to you.

4. If wisdom's ways you'd wisely seek,
    Five things observe with ease;
    Of whom you speak, to whom to speak,
    And how, and when, and where.

Probe and Shed Light

5. Prize your friend for her own true heart,
   Though her dress be poor and mean;
   The years, like a fairy wand, may change
   Cinderella to a queen.

6. We sow a thought and reap an act;
   We sow an act and reap a habit;
   We sow a habit and reap a character;
   We sow a character and reap a destiny. **Thackery**

7. This above all: to thine own self be true;
   And it must follow, as the night the day,
   Thou canst not then be false to any man.
   Shakespeare.

8. He liveth long who liveth well;
   All else in life is thrown away;
   He liveth longest who can tell
   Of true things truly done each day.

9. If you're told to do a thing
   And mean to do it really;
   Never let it be by halves;
   Do it fully, freely! **Phoebe Cary**

10. For want of a nail the shoe was lost;
    For want of a shoe the horse was lost;
    For want of a horse the rider was lost;
    For want of a rider the battle was lost;
       — And all for the want of a horseshoe nail.
    Benjamin Franklin

http://www.rhymes.org.uk/for_want_of_a_nail.htm This online reference to #10 suggests that Mr. Franklin's "For want of a nail" is often used to gently chastise a child whilst explaining the possible events that may follow a thoughtless act. Have family members give examples that reflect its sentiment.

B. **Guiding Lessons**

Use these quotations as guidance for your children, perhaps to stimulate dinner conversations, or for writing essays that use a quote as its theme. Have everyone join in by giving examples that reflect the sentiment of the saying. Discussions about their meanings will enlighten their lives and perhaps help with current problems, injustices, hurts, etc.

A properly chosen one may help a child find his way or "see the light." Consider printing these out in large type to keep near the dinner table. Perhaps you can divide the quotes into groups representative of the ages and abilities of your children and place each into a separate container. Have children take turns drawing a question out of a hat (or whatever), researching the author, and explaining the meaning by giving examples at the next dinner.

1. "Faith, friends, and kindness are beliefs that guide."

2. "People see only what they are prepared to see." **Ralph Waldo Emerson**

3. "I find that the harder I work, the more luck I seem to have." **Thomas Jefferson**

4. "In the End, we will remember not the words of our enemies, but the silence of our friends." **Martin Luther King Jr.**

5. "Whenever I climb I am followed by a dog called 'Ego'." **Friedrich Nietzsche**

6. "Many wealthy people are little more than janitors of their possessions. **Frank Lloyd Wright**

7. "I have not failed. I've just found 10,000 ways that won't work**." Thomas Alva Edison**. Who today could make this statement?

8. "Be nice to people on your way up because you meet them again on your way down." **Jimmy Durante**

9. "I have often regretted my speech, never my silence." **Xenocrates**

10. "Obstacles are those frightful things you see when you take your eyes off your goal." **Henry Ford**

11. "In any contest between power and patience, bet on patience." **W.B. Prescott**

12. "Into each life some rain must fall, some days must be dark and dreary." **Henry Wadsworth Longfellow**

13. "When ideas fail, words come in very handy." **Goethe**

14. "The nice thing about egotists is that they don't talk about other people." **Lucille S. Harper**

15. "I have never let my schooling interfere with my education." **Mark Twain**

16. "A consensus means that everyone agrees to say collectively what no one believes individually." **Abba Eban**

17. "A pessimist sees the difficulty in every opportunity; an optimist sees the opportunity in every difficulty." **Sir Winston Churchill**

18. "The only thing necessary for the triumph of evil is for good men to do nothing." **Edmund Burke**

19. "A pint of sweat saves a gallon of blood." **General George S. Patton**

20. "Whatever is begun in anger ends in shame." **Benjamin Franklin**
    http://quotations.about.com/cs/inspirationquotes/a/Belief7.htm

C.   EXTRAORDINARY ENRICHING EXPERIENCES

It has been widely observed and reported that children enjoy learning when they can think creatively."
J. Richard Suchman

1.   Creative and Constructive Activities for snow and other inclement days!

a. Parents' Role

1. When you get a warning of a big snow headed your way, go to a bank and get either $30 in change (100 pennies, 100 nickels, 50 dimes, 50 quarters, 4 half dollars) or $10 (25 pennies, 20 nickels, 25 dimes, 25 quarters, 2 half-dollars) along with fresh wrappers for each denomination.

2. **Keep the amount secret from the children**! Dump it all into a box.

3. Give each child a paper on which to write his answers.

4. **Supervise**: Sorting, estimating, counting, comparing, researching, writing, working cooperatively

5. **Teach relevant vocabulary**: Denomination, obverse, reverse, motto www.enchantedlearning.com/math/money/coins/penny/

6. **Answer children's questions about various symbols on some coins**: **D** stands for Denver (**ask what state**: Colorado); **P** for Philadelphia (**ask what state**); **S** for San Francisco (**ask what state**). Abraham Lincoln, John F. Kennedy, Franklin D. Roosevelt. **Mottoes** (inspirational messages or emotionally stirring phrases on coins) on current U.S. coins are *Liberty, In God We Trust,* and *E Pluribus Unum* ("out of many, one").

7. **Final tasks:** Check whether children wrote up everything they did and found out!! Oversee children when they put the coins into wrappers.

8. **When the children have finished these, send them out to make a snowman—or measure the rainfall!** You can return

to the bank and get your full investment back. You and your children have already earned plenty of interest!

b. Children's Role

1. Write down your guess of how much money there is. You'll find out later how close you came.

2. Look over the pile of coins. Write down how many pennies, nickels, dimes, quarters, and half dollars you think there are.

3. Now count each of the pennies, nickels, dimes, quarters, and half dollars. How'd you do with your guesses?

4. Can you write five cents three different ways? Check your answer on page 229 of the appendix. Did you get all three?

5. Guess the year on the oldest penny, nickel, dime, quarter, and half dollar. Now sort them out by value and look at the dates on each. If you guessed correctly, you may keep the coin(s) after this activity is finished!

6. What is the total value of each **denomination**? Pennies? Nickels? Dimes? Quarters? Half dollars?

7. Look at the images on front and back (**obverse and reverse sides**) of each coin. How many different types of these did you find: Pennies? Nickels? Dimes? Quarters? Half dollars?

8. Whose images are on the pennies? Nickels? Dimes? Quarters? Half dollars? Use an encyclopedia or the Internet to check your answers.

9. Look for pennies that have a small D or P or S under the date. How many of each did you find? Those letters indicate the city where those coins were **minted** (made). What cities do you think they might be? Write your guesses down. D=? P=? S=? Which mint had the most? Now, go to an encyclopedia or the Internet

to find out which cities the D, P and S stand for. Did you guess them correctly?

10. Does any coin have a saying (**motto**) on it? If yes, what does it say?

11. **Weighing**: If you have a kitchen scale (or better yet, a balance scale), compare weights: How many pennies = a quarter? A nickel? How many dimes does it take to equal the weight of the other coins? How much do ten pennies weigh? Ten nickels? Ten dimes? Ten quarters? Two half-dollars?

12. **Researching**: If you have an encyclopædia or connection to the Internet, look up and write out historical facts concerning those whose images are on a coin: **Abraham Lincoln, John F. Kennedy, Franklin D. Roosevelt**

13. What did Benjamin Franklin mean when he said, "A penny saved is a penny earned."?

14. Now count each of the coins; get a total value for each; get a total for all the coins. Your total should equal $30. Compare answers with original guesses. Unless your count was perfect, dump it all out and start counting all over again!

15. Write up everything you did and what you found out!

16. Now, put the coins into their proper wrappers.

17. Go outside and build a snowman!

2. The Big Sit: An Extra-special Field Trip

> *"As knowledge increases, wonder deepens."*
> **Charles Morgan**

a. **In the Field**: Plan a half-hour "group sit" on a grassy hill adjacent to a busy highway or in a building that looks out over a highway. Outfit everyone with a small notebook and pencil. This outing will provide

participants with counting and graphing exercises, working with percentages, researching, learning new words* —and having fun!
*See below

Before heading out to the viewing spot, have each child choose a color (or draw one from a container) of a car and guess how many cars will have that color. Once seated above the highway, they will begin to tally their cars' colors. Teach children to count their colors by making hatch/hash/tick marks (notations) in groups of five for each car of the relevant color, so that when the activity is over, they can quickly find their totals.

b. Take the information home to discover:
  1. The total number of vehicles recorded.
  2. Which color was most prevalent?
  3. What percentage of the total did each color represent?

c. **And when there's a lull in the traffic, make words from license plates' letters.** If they have 3 letters together, try to make a word that uses those letters **in the order in which they appear**. You may add letters in front of those on the plate, as long as you keep them in the right order, and the same letters may be used more than once. This activity provides thinking, learning, and fun.

Of course, you can do this at other times, whether you're taking a walk or are off somewhere in your car. You can make this a family exercise, or you can gather into teams with others. Here are ten examples to give you practice, with a few possibilities included for the first three:

RPD: rapid, torpid, ripped; _____
LGN: legend, leggings, laughing;_____
TPR: taper, tapir, stapler; _____
SPN: _____
PCE: _____
ETR: _____
PLS: _____
SDE: _____
PCH: _____

d. Expand learning on another day by counting other types of vehicles. Assign one type to each participant.

1. Two-door vs four-door cars
2. SUVs vs sedans: Do they know what SUV means? (Sport Utility Vehicle)
3. Motorcycles
4. Convertibles
5. Station wagons

e.  Before counting trucks, have children learn the various types and purposes of the vehicles that make up this category: light weight, heavy weight, eight-wheelers. They can go through magazines, download images from the Internet, draw various types, visit a nearby Interstate truck stop, take pictures of trucks and label each type and more!

1. Decide beforehand what constitutes a truck: Van? Pick-up? Flatbed?
2. Learn what to call the various types of trucks: Semi-trailers; tank trucks; cement mixers; moving vans...
3. Figure the percentage of trucks to other vehicles.

f. Take a trip to an RV showroom or a trailer park so children can examine vehicles up close. Encourage them to measure the length of different ones and to take brochures home with further information.

g. At home:

1. Go online or to an encyclopædia to learn about vehicles in other countries. For instance, a German "recreational vehicle" is called "Wohnmobil." Wohnen means to live or reside. A Spanish RV is called a autocaravana or "Casa Rodante" (Rolling House). Help children find these and other countries on a world map or atlas.

A **rickshaw/auto rickshaw** for hire is one of the chief modes of transport in India, Pakistan, Nepal, Bangladesh, the Philippines, Sri Lanka, and Sudan, and is popular elsewhere. Rickshaws, three-wheeled carts often pulled by a man, have a tin/iron body resting on three small wheels (one in front, two on the rear). Motorized rickshaws have a small cabin in the front for the driver (called an *auto-wallah* in some areas) and seating for three in the rear. Today there are motorized versions of the traditional rickshaw. Encourage children to draw pictures of rickshaws.

2. Make a scrapbook of different types of vehicles; label each.

3. Write an essay on which type of vehicle you like best /would like to own and explain why.

4. Research, explore, draw recreational vehicles (RVs)

   a. Which vehicles fall into this category?

   b. What do the A, B, C classes of these vehicles mean?

   c. What are RVs' different uses? (offices, camping and ???)

   d. Discuss the advantages of RVs. The disadvantages.

   e. Which US city is known as the "RV Capital of the World"? [Elkhart, Indiana] Why?

   f. What does a British Caravan mean? [travel trailer]

   g. What is a 4 x 4?

   h. What does the **T** in ATV mean? (terrain; what does this mean?)

   i. What is a "Winnebago?" [A popular brand of recreational vehicle, named after the Native American tribes of Nebraska,

Iowa and Wisconsin] The generic term given to many similar vehicles made by other companies.

h. Study Other Vehicles

1. Motor homes
2. Trailers: Camping, Toy Haulers, horse
3. Buses
4. Explain vehicles' names: Viper, Prowler, etc.

i. Learn the Language of Vehicles

1. **axle** (n): A supporting shaft or member on or with which a wheel or a set of wheels revolves

2. **chassis** (n): The rectangular steel frame, supported on springs and attached to the axles, that holds the body and motor of an automobile

3. **commercial** (adj): A vehicle used for the buying and selling of goods. What types can you name? [mail, UPS, FedEx, telephone repair ...]

4. **compact car**: Small. Occupying little space compared with other cars. How many compact models can you name? See online site in Appendix page 229.

5. **coupé** (n) (pronounced coo pay), from French meaning to cut. Coupés are two-door cars, usually with only two seats (as though they were **cut** from a full-size vehicle); many have a hatchback (see 12 below) instead of a trunk.

6. **customize** (v): Make to specifications or requirements. What can a buyer or owner of a car customize?

7. **cab** (n): The covered compartment of a heavy vehicle, such as a truck, in which the driver sits

8. **compact** (adj): A small car. What are the advantages of one?

9. **convertible** (adj/n): A car that has a top that can be folded or removed. It coverts (changes) from one kind of vehicle to another. Why do people buy these?

10. **conveyance** (n): Something that serves as a means of transportation. How many can you name? [Car, taxi, wagon, trucks of different sizes and purposes]. What is an air-cushion vehicle? (Answer on page in Appendix on page 229)

11. **diesel** (adj): An internal-combustion engine that burns heavy oil (n): A type of oil.

12. **fifth wheel** (n): An expression meaning an extra and unnecessary person or thing, originating from an additional wheel carried on a four-wheeled vehicle as a spare. Would you want to be a fifth wheel? Should you call anyone else a fifth wheel? Why or why not?

13. **hatchback**: An automobile having a sloping back with a hatch that opens upward.

14. **minivan** (adj: small + van)

15. **petroleum** ("rock oil;" a naturally occurring, flammable liquid found in rock formations). It is often abbreviated to "petro."

16. **sedan** (n): A passenger car with two rows of seats and a trunk. A sedan in England is called a *saloon* and its trunk is a *boot*.

17. **subcompact** (adj/n): Smaller than a compact car. We bought a subcompact.

18. **SUV**: Sports Utility Vehicle. **utility** (adj): Useful. I took my utility knife along in my utility vehicle. (n): The quality of being of practical use. Besides a Sports Utility Vehicle, what other utility vehicles can you name? [Vehicles designed for specific services and uses: telephone trucks; carpenters' vans]

19. **vehicle** (n) (from the Latin *vehiculum*): A conveyance that transports people or objects

3. Home-Schooling

"The cure for boredom is curiosity. There is not cure for curiosity."
Dorothy Parker

a. Become a Climatologist: Keep track of the weather!

Use graph paper to show daily temperatures and precipitation. At the end of the month, circle the days that had the highest temperature and the lowest, the most rain or snow. What were they? If you do not have an outdoor thermometer or a rain gauge, go to http://vp.accuweather.com/vantagepoint/wx/past_climo and type in your town or city. You will find both the daily information and the whole month's. Compare months to each other. Which was the wettest? Compare each year's total to previous years.

If you have a friend who lives in a different area, compare your findings.

FARMERS' WEATHERWISE SAYINGS

"Swallows flying way up high   *Swallows flying near the ground*
Mean there's no rain in the sky.   *Mean a storm will come around.*

"When the dew is on the grass   *When grass is dry at morning light*
Rain will never come to pass.   *Look for rain before the night.'*

b. Discharge Domestic Duties

Compute your newspapers' and store flyers' information on sales' discounts; your bank's savings account interest; rate of borrowing from a bank.

1. When instructions for heating or cooking an item call for 1½ minutes in the microwave, what numbers do you push on the key pad?_____ What about 2¼ minutes?_____ Three hours?_____ Three-and-a half hours? _____ Continue to practice with different times until you become proficient.

2. Guess weights of various fruits and vegetables. Use a kitchen balance or digital scale for the answers, or measure heaviness of various quantities of fruits and veggies in a grocery store. If you have a bathroom scale, you can figure out the weight of anything that weighs over a pound by weighing yourself first without the item and then with it and subtracting the difference. A balance scale would be helpful for weighing apples and apples or apples and oranges.

   a. One apple, two apples, five apples …
   b. One banana, two …
   c. One orange, two oranges....
   d. A handful of grapes or cherries
   e. One potato, two …
   f. A head of lettuce
   g. Various numbers of tomatoes

c. Convert Measurements

1. If your scales show weights in grams or ounces, you can learn the relationship between the two. Double the numbers shown here for heavier weights. If you start with 1 oz.=2.834 grams, you can covert any number of ounces to grams.
2. Other measurements may need converting, too. Below are related sites that deal with converting measurements of gardens to specifications for mulch or for the number

of plants that will fit into a designated garden, as well as practice with metric measures.

http://pss.uvm.edu/pss123/gardenmath.htm
http://pss.uvm.edu/pss123/equivtab.htm
http://www.nist.gov/public_affairs/kids/metric.htm
http://sciencespot.net/Pages/classmetric.html
http://www.emints.org/ethemes/resources/S00000356.
shtml
http://www.aaamath.com/mea.html
http://themathworksheetsite.com/subscr/english_metric_
conversions.html

d. Get Familiar With Various Measures

1. Make up orders, fill out forms in mail order catalogues or make online "orders"; total the amounts and weights of your "purchases." (Children 3rd grade+)

2. Use a road map. Ask an adult to make up a set of questions about distances between two or more places on the map. Can you find more than one way to get from point A to point B? Which is shorter in miles? Which would probably take less time? Why?

3. Take a fantasy journey from your home to a particular place anywhere in this hemisphere. Make a list of all the places you would like to stop en route and then, using an atlas, put those stops in geographical order — the order in which you would make your visit. Then, figure the total distance you'd travel by adding the miles or kilometers together between each stop. What would the distance be for a round trip?

4. Learn to estimate the distance of a mile; a half a mile; five miles when you're in a car. Compare the car's odometer to your calculations. Repeat until you're right on the button.

5. Guess the measurements of all sorts of things in your home in both metrics and American (standard/English) measures:

The area of the living room for wall-to-wall carpeting; the perimeter of the room for new molding to go all around the top of the room; the area of all the doors in a room so as to order paint to cover them. How close did your guesses come after you made the measurements?

0   12345 67890   5

e.   **Decode the 12-digit Universal Product Code** (UPC) bar codes on various items, such as food products and some pieces of clothing. Use the four pages of http://www.howstuffworks.com/upc.htm to find out what each digit on a product means.

f.   **Become A Smart Shopper**

1.   Compute the savings on sale items as advertised in current or past grocery ads versus the regular price. Add up a shopping trip's savings. Compare sale prices of several similar products. (Children 3rd grade+)

2.   Improve your shopping smarts by using store ads, often in weekend newspapers, to make up a real or pretend shopping list. Find the items' total. Here's a list for you to work on:

   a.   Sweet rolls, 10 for $10. How much is each roll?
   b.   Cans of dog food, 2 for $1. How much is each can? How much are 5 cans? Ten cans? and so on.
   c.   Ice cream cartons, 2 for $5; 3 for ?$
   d.   Box of popsicles, 2 for $6; 4 for ?$
   e.   Cans of cat food, 10 for $3; 25 for ?$
   f.   Jars of pasta sauce, 3 for $5; 9 for ?$
   g.   Cans of tuna, 8 for $10; 4 for ? How many can you buy for $20?
   h.   Jars of juice, 3 for $4; 6 for ?$; 12 for ?

What change will you expect to get from $20? $30? etc.

3. Do the math on ads for fruit by becoming familiar with those that are in season, and those that are not, as well as what amounts the ads represent. For instance, out-of-season berries and other fruits are often marketed in quarter-pound amounts, making them seem like a very good buy, whereas, in-season ones might sell a whole pound for the same price.

4. Practice this little-known money-saver in a grocery store: Compare prices of two or more sizes of the same product by reading the cost per pound that is on a small tag below the product. Often the smaller boxes or bags prove to be better buys than the bigger ones! Teach your friends!

NOW THAT YOU HAVE DONE ALL THE WORK IN THIS BOOK, IT'S TIME TO TAKE A HOLIDAY! WHERE WILL YOU GO? WHAT WILL YOU DO?

See Page 234 in Appendix

SAGE EDUCATION ENTERPRISES PRODUCTS Page 238 in Appendix

HOMESCHOOLING REFERENCES

http://www.americanhomeschoolassociation.org/: American Home School
    Association:
http://www.nhen.org/: National Home Education Network:
HomeEdMag@aol.com
http://www.homeschoolnewslink.com/
http://www.learningthings.com/
http://www.teachingtools.com/
http://www.laurelsprings.com/ (Distance learning)
http://www.oakmeadow.com/ (Distance learning)
http://schooloftomorrow.com/Default.asp (Distance learning)
http://www.sycamoretree.com (Distance learning)

ADDITIONAL REFERENCES FOR TEACHERS AND STUDENTS

http://kids.discovery.com/
http://disney.go.com/index
http://www.kidwings.com/index.htm
http://www.dmoz.org/Kids_and_Teens/
http://pbskids.org/
http://www.google.com/search?hl=en&q=kathy+schrock&aq=7&oq=KATHY
http://kids.nationalgeographic.com/
http://www2.scholastic.com/browse/home.jsp
http://www.smithsonianeducation.org/
http://www.google.com/search?hl=en&q=time+for+kids&btnG=Search
http://kids.yahoo.com/
http://grammar.ccc.commnet.edu/grammar/

AFTERWORD

Ever since my own children were little, I have found that it is easy to interest children in just about anything, so working with them in a variety of ways has been one of the greatest joys of my life. I hope that I'll be able to share fun and knowledge with children and parents for many years to come.

Gaining understanding of the learning process is ongoing for me, and one in which I revel. I hope to continue to find more ways to help children master material which they find difficult.

And …since you have accessed this book by one means or another, I'd be pleased if you would contact me with comments or questions. elinormiller@ seepub.com. Put "book" or "teacher" in the subject line, so I can pull your email out of my spam.

APPENDIX

CHAPTER ONE

Acronyms
>   **TEXACO:** Texas Company
>   **HOV:** High Occupancy Vehicles
>   **TGIF:** Thank Goodness It's Friday!
>   **HAZMAT:** Hazardous Materials

>   **a.**   He made it clear <u>not to</u> cross the white line.
>   **b.**   The balloon began to drop <u>slowly</u>.
>   **c.**   He went to call his daughter frantically. **OR,** Frantically, he went to call his daughter

Automobiles' cognomens

>   **Cabriolet:** A vehicle with a top that folded back; a convertible, formerly a small two-wheeled horse-drawn carriage; with two seats and a folding hood
>   **(Chevy) Caprice:** An abrupt change in feeling, opinion or action or fancy; a fantastic notion
>   **Envoy:** A representative of a government who is sent on a special diplomatic mission
>   **(Dodge) Intrepid:** Fearless, bold, courageous
>   **(Oldsmobile) Intrigue:** A plot to gain a desired end; a secret and illicit affair
>   **Legacy:** Money or property bequeathed to another by will; something handed down from an ancestor
>   **Odyssey:** A long, wandering travel, from the ten-year-long voyage of Ulysses/Odysseus

Sports Teams

>   **1.   Baltimore Orioles**: This bird "wears" the orange and black colors of Lord Baltimore, one of the founding fathers of Maryland.

Probe and Shed Light

2. **Dallas Mavericks:** A maverick is a dissenter, one who refuses to abide by the dictates of group. An unbranded range animal, especially a calf that has become separated from its mother, is traditionally considered the property of the first person who brands it, but ... a certain Sam Maverick made a practice of not branding his calves, so his name became attached to anyone who was one who doesn't do what others do.

3. **Detroit Pistons:** Pistons are part of a car's engine, and Detroit is the car-making center of our country.

4. **Green Bay Packers:** There was a large meat packing industry in Green Bay.

5. **New York Knickerbockers**: Knickerbockers, the old Dutch settlers of New York, wore a style of pants gathered at the knees, often abbreviated to "knickers." Golfers often wear knickers.

6. **Orlando Magic:** Disney's Magic Mountain is in Orlando.

7. **Philadelphia 76ers:** The Declaration of Independence was signed in Philadelphia in 1776.

8. **Pittsburgh Steelers:** Pittsburgh, once known as the Steel Capital of the World, still has a large steel industry.

9. **San Diego Padres:** San Diego was first settled by the Spanish missionaries, called padres (fathers).

10. **Utah Jazz:** This team was originally formed in New Orleans, Louisiana, a city described as the birthplace of jazz. The team moved from New Orleans to Utah. Utah is not known for jazz music.

Because I believe that homeschooling families maintain wholesome, what others might think are old-fashioned, values, I include here the titles of the songs from which we chose each day to end our morning assembly and which I consider to be fundamental to our culture. It would be nice when groups of homeschoolers get together if they chose some of these songs to sing together. These, I am sure, are all online.

Probe and Shed Light

PATRIOTIC SONGS

America
America the Beautiful
Anchors Aweigh
The Caissons Go Rolling Along
Columbia, the Gem of the Ocean
God Bless America
Grand Old Flag
Marine Hymn
Maryland, My Maryland
The Star Spangled Banner
This Land is Your Land
When Johnny Comes Marching Home Again
U. S. Airforce Song "Off we go ..."
Yankee Doodle
Yankee Doodle-Oodle, a college parody

OLD FAVORITES

A capital ship (for an ocean trip ...)
The ants come marching one by one
Are you sleeping? (Frère Jacques) (a round)
As I walked out in the streets of Laredo
The big rock candy mountain
Billy boy (21 verses)
Bought me a cat
Bound for the promised land
The Camptown races
Cielito lindo in English & Spanish (beautiful heaven)
Clementine
Come, follow (round)
Corn cobs twist your hair (old Yankee song to the tune of Yankee Doodle)
          "Corn cobs twist your hair,
          Cart wheels run round you,
          Fiery dragons take you off,
          And mortal pestal pound you."

[For more information on this strange but historic song, see:
http://xroads.virginia.edu/~HYPER/rourke/ch01.html]

Crooked little man
Daisy Bell (Bicycle build for two)
Davy Crockett
Deep in the heart of Texas
Dixie Land (I wish I was in the land of cotton...)
Down in the valley
Erie canal
For he's a jolly good fellow
Frankie and Johnny (28 verses)
Grandfather's clock
Hinky-dinky, parlee-voo!
Home on the range
I don't want to play in your yard
I'm looking over a four-leaf clover
I've been working on the railroad
Jeanie with the light brown hair
John Brown's body
John Peel
Juanita
The keeper (did a shooting go)
Lavender's blue
Loch Lomond
Lou'siana gals (Buffalo gals)
O, no John
Oh, bury me not on the lone prairie
Oh! Susanna
Old folks at home
Old gray mare
On top of Old Smokey
On top of spaghetti (to the tune above)
Oranges and lemons (say the bells of St. Clemens)
Red River Valley
The riddle song (I gave my love a cherry ...)
She'll be comin' 'round the mountain
Shenandoah
Simple gifts

Probe and Shed Light

Sweet Betsy from Pike
Sweetly sings the donkey (round)
(There is a) Tavern in the town
Tell me why (the stars do shine)
There's hole in my bucket (19 verses)
This old man
Waltzing Matilda
When I first came to this land

*http://xroads.virginia.edu/~HYPER/rourke/ch01.html
https://jscholarship.library.jhu.edu/handle/1774.2/14654

Answers to Ripped From the Press, page 34

a.   I never saw a bit of a problem between **he** or his wife. (Correction: ...between **him** and his wife)

b.   I wanted to see if anyone's interests would be **peaked**. (Correction: peaked should have been "piqued.")

c.   Both **her** and her husband forgot about it. (Correction: ...**she** and her husband...)

d.   There's several things in there that indicate to **myself** and the district attorney that suggest mental health issues. (Corrections: **There's** should be there are; **myself** should be me, a frequent misuse.)

e.   Every one of us has done something **they** regret. (Correction: Every one is singular; they, referring back to every one is plural.)

f.   Help needed finding **critically missing** man. (Correction: What is critical?)

MORE APHORISMS from page 68.

I suggest selecting one of these below to be used as a teaching moment or as a topic to discuss during dinner. Can your children explain the meaning of these sayings?

"Action is the antidote to despair." **Joan Baez**

"A man of knowledge lives by acting, not by thinking about acting**." Carlos Casteneda**

"An eye for eye only ends up making the whole world blind." **Mahatma Gandhi**

"A pint of sweat saves a gallon of blood." **General George S. Patton**

"A real friend is one who walks in when the rest of the world walks out." **Walter Winchell**

"Asking a question is only embarrassing just for that moment. Not asking is embarrassing and it will haunt you for the rest of your life." **Japanese Proverb**

"Do not go where the path may lead; go instead where there is no path and leave a trail." **Ralph Waldo Emerson**

"Facts are the enemy of truth." **Don Quixote**, *Man of La Mancha*

"Faith and doubt cannot exist in the same mind at the same time, for one will dispel the other**." Stephen L Richards**

"Faith is to believe what we do not see; the reward of faith is to see what we believe." **Saint Augustine** (354-430)

"Faith without works is like a bird without wings; though she may hop with her companions on earth, yet she will never fly with them to heaven." **Francis Beaumont**

"Facts are the enemy of truth." Don Quixote, Man of La Mancha

"Friendship without self-interest is one of the rare and beautiful things of life." **James Francis Byrnes**

"I fear we are too much concerned with material things to remember that our real strength

"If we thought twice about everything we say, perhaps we would only say half as much." **Ben Franklin**

"I look to a day when people will not be judged by the color of their skin, but by the content of their character." **Martin Luther King, Jr.**

"It's easier to be done than to be satisfied." **Quincy Jones**

"It is harder to crack a prejudice than an atom." **Albert Einstein**

"Lead the life that will make you kindly and friendly to everyone about you, and you will be surprised what a happy life you will lead." **Charles M. Schwab**

"Life is God's gift to man. What we do with our life is our gift to God." **Harold B. Lee**

"Never look down on anybody unless you're helping him up**." Jesse Jackson**

"One of the secrets of life is to make stepping-stones out of stumbling blocks." **Jack Penn**

"Some men see things as they are and ask why. Others dream things that never were and ask why not." B

"Spiritual values transcend the material artifacts that we can touch and see. They take us into the realm of beauty, inspiration and love." **Nido Qubein**

"Success seems to be connected with action. Successful people keep moving. They make mistakes but they never quit." **Conrad Hilton**

"The greatest pleasure I know is to do a good action by stealth, and to have it found out by accident." **Charles Lamb** (1775-1834)

"The reason a dog has so many friends is that he wags his tail instead of his tongue." **Anonymous**

"Two roads diverged in a wood, and I, I took the one less traveled by**." Robert Frost**

"Unless you try to do something beyond what you have already mastered, you will never grow." **Walter Winchell**

"We evaluate others with a Godlike justice, but we want them to evaluate us with a Godlike compassion." **Sydney J. Harris**

"We judge ourselves mostly by our intentions, but others judge us mostly by our actions." **Eric Harvey and Alexander D. Lucia**

"Well-timed silence hath more eloquence than speech." **Martin F. Tupper**

Answers to Proverbs in Book:

2. two
3. link
6. are
12. not
18. until/before

MORE ADAGES AND PROVERBS: I suggest selecting these below for teaching moments or as topics to discuss during dinner. Can your children explain the meaning of these sayings?

A bird in hand is worth two in the bush.

A journey of a thousand miles begins with a single step.

As The Tree Grows, So The Twig is Bent

Average minds discuss events. Small minds discuss people.

Believe in yourself! Have faith in your abilities! Without a humble but reasonable confidence in your own powers, you cannot be successful or happy.

Can't change yesterday, can't predict tomorrow, so try and live today like it is the first or last day of your life.

Do something nice for somebody, anybody, simply because you can.

Even a small thorn causes festering.

Fools rush ___ where angels fear to tread.*1

God gave people a mouth that closes and ears that don't, which should tell us something."

God helps them ___ help themselves.*2

Good friends are hard to find, harder to leave, and impossible to forget

Have confidence in your own powers, you cannot be successful or happy.

He who asks is a fool for five minutes, but he who does not ask remains a fool forever.

He who laughs last laughs best.

I don't know the key to success, but the key to failure is to try to please everyone.

If a man deceives me once, shame on him; if he deceives me twice, shame on me.

If you believe everything you read, better not read.

If you buy what you do not need, you will need what you cannot buy.

It is no use crying ___ spilt milk.*3

It is not fish until it is on the bank. (See, "Don't count your chickens ....)

It was the last straw.

Judge not lest ye be judged.

Kind words can be short and easy to speak but their echoes are endless.

Make hay while the sun shines.

Necessity is the ___ of invention.*4

No pain, ___ gain.*5

Once burned, twice shy

One of these days is none of these days.

Rats desert a sinking ship.

Remember that not getting what you want is sometimes a wonderful stroke of luck.

Rome was not built in a day.

Still waters run ___.*6

Take thy thoughts to bed with thee, for the morning is wiser than the evening.

The best things in life aren't things.

The first step is the hardest.

The last straw breaks the camel's ___. *7

The tongue is more to be feared than the sword.

The ___ step is the hardest.*8

There's no ___ without fire.*9

Things done by halves are never done well.

Those who live in glass houses should not ___ stones.*10

Though a tree grows ever so high, the falling leaves return to the ground.

To teach is to learn.

Tomorrow is often the busiest day of the week.

Probe and Shed Light

Too ___ cooks spoil the broth.*11

Truth stands the test of time; lies are soon exposed. *Proverbs* 12:19

Unless you try to do something beyond what you have already mastered, you will
never grow.

Waste not, ___ not.*12

We don't find friends; we make them.

What breaks in a moment may take years to mend.

When one dog barks, another will join it.

When the cat's away, the ___ will play.*13

When there is no enemy within, the enemies outside cannot hurt you.

Who knows most speaks least.

You can lead a horse to water, but you cannot make him drink.

You can't tell a ___ by its cover.*14

C. ANSWERS TO PROVERBS' MISSING WORDS

*1. in
*2. who
*3. over
*4. mother
*5. no
*6.deep
*7 back
*8. first
*9. smoke
*10. throw
*11. many
*12. want
*13. mice
*14. Book

D. ANSWERS TO LITERARY ALLUSIONS

11. To cry wolf: **a**. to give alarm without occasion
12. A Simon Legree: **a**. a cruel taskmaster
13. To tilt at windmills: **b**. to fight imaginary enemies
14. A pig in a poke: **b**. something whose true value is unknown
15. To run with the hare and hunt with the hounds: a. to keep in favor with
    both parties to an argument

E. ANSWERS TO SYNONYMS

4. **helpful—useful/beneficial/advantageous**
5. **mad/furious/enraged—angry**

F. ANSWERS TO ANAGRAMS

17. they see
18. best in prayer
19. Genuine class
20. Detect thieves

G. From Page 77: Game Theory

Chicken: Derived from the game in which two drivers race toward each other to see who will swerve first. This game is one in which neither player wants to yield to the other—even when a "collision" is the worst possible outcome. In science fields such as biology, this game is known as the Hawk-Dove game.

Stag Hunt: Also known as the assurance game. This game involves making a choice between individual safety and risky cooperation. The idea behind this game—involving two hunters who must decide whether to hunt a hare alone or a stag together—was developed by the philosopher Jean-Jacques Rousseau.

Prisoner's Dilemma: A famous situation and perhaps the most important in all of game theory. This game involves two prisoners being separately interrogated for their common crime. Each must decide whether to confess or remain silent, knowing his partner has the same choice. If neither confesses, they each get a one-year sentence.

If both confess, each gets three years. And if only one confesses, he goes free, but sends his partner away for five years.

http://www.gametheory.net/
http://william-king.www.drexel.edu/top/eco/game/game.html

CHILDREN'S ROLE: CREATIVE AND CONSTRUCTIVE ACTIVITIES FOR SNOW DAYS: Answer to #4 (page 202): 5¢ or .05 or $0.05.

Answers to a big-sit question, page 208

Probe and Shed Light

1. **Air-cushion vehicle**: A hovercraft, a vehicle that is supported above the surface of land or water by a cushion of air produced by downwardly directed fans

2. **A few compact models**: **Chevy**: Aveo, Cobalt; **Hyundai**: Genesis Coupe Accent; **Volkswagen** Jetta. For more go to:
   http://www.automotive.com/new-cars/27/compact/index.html

Fibonacci Mathematics From Page 130
http://www.mcs.surrey.ac.uk/Personal/R.Knott/Fibonacci/
http://www.gap-system.org/~history/Mathematicians/Fibonacci.html

Think of a number between 1 and 10. Triple it. Add 6. Then triple again. Now take your answer, probably a two-digit number, and add the digits of your answer. If you still have a two-digit number, add those digits again. You should now be thinking of the magical number 9. The reason this works is based on algebra and the fact that the digits of any multiple of 9 must sum to a multiple of 9.

The Fibonacci sequence shows up in many spheres of mathematics, as well as in nature, art, computer science, and poetry. I think Fibonacci is fun; (please keep the format of the next 4 lines]
We start with a 1 and a 1.
Then 2, 3, 5, 8,
But don't stop there, mate!
The fun has just barely begun.
The series continues on: 13, 21, 34, 55, 89, ... with each successive Fibonacci number being the sum of the previous two. This simple pattern is named for a 12th-century mathematician who described a problem involving imaginary rabbits that never die. Starting with a pair of baby rabbits, the animals take a month to mature, then mate and produce a male and a female; these mature after a month and mate, along with their parents. The total number of pairs after each month follows the Fibonacci sequence.

In our own day, Fibonacci numbers appear as a critical plot element in *The Da Vinci Code*, notably under the guise of the golden ratio, an ideal proportion favored by artists and architects that is intimately connected to the Fibonacci sequence.

For the First Time in History, Time Mattered (from page 161).

The hourglass and mechanical clock were invented during the plague years. Labor was suddenly valuable and had to be measured. Wealth was expected to grow and time was critical in understanding the productivity that determined growth. It is no accident that Adam Smith and his definition of Capitalism arrived at the end of the plague. This change in the relationship between time and humankind had long lasting affects on the world. In pre-plague Europe the time measuring device was the sundial. In fact, by the 10th century, pocket sundials were commonplace. A pocket sundial is very helpful if you want to know if it is morning, afternoon, or night. But accuracy past those delineations of the day is pretty illusive in such a crude device. In post-plague Europe, where time became money, the mechanical clock became the king.

The transition between sundial and clock involved an also-ran technology - the hourglass. It is strange to think of the hourglass and the mechanical clock as sharing, more or less the same historical period for their origins. The hourglass seems ancient. The clock seems such a device of the Industrial Age.

The hourglass is imprecise. The sand never pours through the opening at the same rate. So, successive hours tend to have significant variance in their length. Hours of the dry winter were shorter than hours of the humid summer. The hourglass worked well wherever a gauge was needed to block off large, sloppy units of time.

Step away from the functionality of the hourglass and see it as a symbol. The hourglass represents man's former, church-centered relationship with time - pessimistic, inevitable, unyielding. God owned time. Man responded to God. Remember the European icon of death? It is a skeleton wearing a monk's robe, carrying what? A scythe to remind you that you will be cut down and an hourglass to remind you that time is both short and unrelenting. For all of its seven-hundred years the hourglass has been a universal symbol of death and hopelessness.

The mechanical clock, however, embodied a new way of viewing man's relationship with time - predictable, reliable, ordered and certain. In post-plague Europe, man controls time. The clock - metaphor speaks to a universe that will be discovered by humankind rather than revealed by God.

Killing Time In Our Own Time

Now, there is a new clock in town. This time it is biological, not mechanical. Early evidence is that this clock is a time-killer. The invention of this new clock began fifty years ago when Watson and Crick discovered the double helix structure of human DNA. That gigantic scientific step ultimately launched the human genome project that is identifying all the constituent pieces of human DNA. It is pretty exciting. Science may be on the threshold of curing and preventing major diseases and birth defects. Who does not want to rid the world of cancer and AIDS, heart disease, diabetes, cystic fibrosis, and spinal bifita? This is a wonderful and powerful path for humanity. There is, however, a branch of this path that may not be so wonderful. It presents humans with a choice that will define just how selfish we may be. It has to do with aging and that, of course, has to do with time. Biologists think of aging very differently than most of us. They measure age based upon how many times a cell divides during its life.

Human cells divide about 70 times before they die. They die because they wear out in a mechanical sense. At the ends of chromosomes that carry the genetic material of the cell are protective caps called telomeres. Each time a cell divides, parts of the telomeres are lost and the structures fray a little. Eventually, telomeres become too short to protect the genes, the genetic material is damaged during cell division and the cell dies.

Three years ago a joint U.S. and Canadian team used this knowledge and the early results of the human genome project to create an experiment that would stop the aging process. Six cows in Connecticut had their aging genes extracted. These cows have not aged since those genes were removed. Their telomeres have not been damaged during cell division.

Such cloning and aging theory may lead to treatments that enable a patient's own tissue to be used to grow compatible transplant tissue—tissue that, by the way, would be young. We may be on the verge of a giant breakthrough on the diseases of aging such as heart disease, arthritis and possibly even Alzheimer's.

That is the good news about this path. The unsettling news is that it may be possible to scale up this anti-aging phenomenon to an entire organism. If so, humans who have their aging genes extracted might have a natural life span of between 120 to 200 years.

It is unlikely that you will soon see a TV infomercial or a doctor's ad hawking such an anti-aging procedure the way they do for Viagra, or Rogaine. Tough technical and ethical questions lie ahead. However, think how tempting it will be to focus a significant part of the medical dollar away from the relief of suffering and toward the extension of life. The end of Ponce De Leon's search for the fountain of youth may be coming to a successful, albeit unexpected kind of end.

Where do children fit in a world where telomeres never wear out, and the genes of aging can be extracted from a person? Do children fit in at all? When faced with the choice between the lengthy, high-quality extension of your own life and bringing another generation of humankind into the world, how would you choose?

Six-hundred years from now, will children still sing about the Black Plague in their nursery rhyme? Or, as humans vanquish disease and kill time, will the children change their tune?

We are nose-to-nose with one of the big questions of human existence. Does the ultimate value lie in the human individual or in the human race? I don't have the answer, but one way or another, time will tell.

G. William Troxler, Ph.D.
© 2001 G. William Troxler All rights reserved

Books

In Search of the Dark Ages, by Michael Wood. This book was a companion to a television series by the same name. It provides an excellent look at the world just prior to the plague. Facts On File Publications, New York, 1987.

Civilization, by Kenneth Clark. Another companion book for a PBS series and one of the first such texts to be written, this book uses the visual arts to explain history. Harper & Row, New York, 1969

Consilience, by Edward O. Wilson. This is a wonderful intellectual romp by one of the world's greatest living scientists. His aim is to provide a case for the fundamental unity of all knowledge. As the founder of the socio-biology movement, he brings a particularly timely perspective to the subject.

Links and Images

http://english.ttu.edu/grad/Geiger/Summer98/Project2/Plague.html
http://english.ttu.edu/grad/Geiger/Summer98/Project2/Plague.html
A quick overview of the medieval Black Plague period with attention focused on authors - especially Chaucer.
http://www.allsands.com/History/Events/blackplaguebub_eq_gn.htm
An excellent and thorough history of the Black Plague.

From page 167: Height of an average horse is between 14 and 18 hands in height, though some breeds are smaller than that.

From page 169: Light travels at **11,176,944 miles per minute; 670,616,629 miles per hour.**

Cryptogram , page 174: Take life as you find it, but don't leave it that way.

Mathematical Progressions page 177

    a. (9 11 13 15; **b.** D23 E22 F21; **c.** 2 32 2; d. WD VE UF; **e.** 20 26 33;

    f. P V C; **g.** 1/12 1/14 1/16 **h.** D Q E

    i. (3 x 2 +1 = 7; 7 x 2 + 1= 15; 15 x 2 + 1; **63; 127**

    j. SEVEN

    k. THREE

    l. 21 + 13 = **34**; 13 + 34 = **55**; 55 + 34 = **79** ; **m. +20 = 2000**

Alphametics/Cryptarithm : Pages 178

4. a. BOY	306	**4. b.** SEND	9576	4c. WRONG	25938
x 25	25	x MORE	1085	WRONG	25938
ARBO	**1530**	**MONEY**	**10652**	**R I G H T**	**51876**

	HOE	1 8 5
HEN) LOVES	3 9 4) 7 2 8 9 5
I L L	3 9 4
I OE	3 3 4 9
HEN	3 1 5 2
HNIS	1 9 7 5
HHLS	1 9 7 0
RS	5

Math Master: I'm thinking of a number: page 180-181

    a. 1: 45; 2: 63; 3: 84; 4: 60; 5: 72

    b. **5188**

    c. **93**

NOW THAT YOU HAVE DONE ALL THE WORK IN THIS BOOK, IT'S TIME TO TAKE A HOLIDAY! WHERE WILL YOU GO? WHAT WILL YOU DO?

JANUARY

January 1st: **New Year's Day**,

Third Monday in January: **Birthday of Martin Luther King**.

January 20th every four years, starting in 1937: **Inauguration Day** [1]

Late January or February (date varies): **Chinese New Year**: The start of the New Year in the lunar calendar, often associated with China or other Asian nations and a time to celebrate their cultures.

FEBRUARY

Black History Month: Celebrating the contributions and culture of Afro Americans (Black Americans; U.S. Citizens descended from Africans)

Third Monday in February since 1971: **Presidents' Day.** Prior to that year, it celebrated **Washington's Birthday** on the traditional date of February 22.

February 2: **Groundhog Day**. Prediction from Punxsutawney, Pennsylvania, groundhog (Punxsutawney Phil) on whether the country will have six more weeks of winter

February 12: **Lincoln's Birthday**

February 14: **Valentine's Day**

February or March, date varies: **Mardi Gras and Ash Wednesday**—A festive season (Carnival) leading up to Shrove Tuesday or Mardi Gras. Closes with Ash Wednesday (40 days before Easter, not counting Sundays), which starts the season of Lent in the Christian calendar.

MARCH

March 4th: every four years: **Inauguration Day**

March 17: **St. Patrick's Day**: A celebration of Irish heritage and culture, based on the Catholic feast of St. Patrick. Primary activity is simply the wearing of green clothing ("wearing o' the green"), although drinking beer dyed green is also popular. Attending St. Patrick's Day parades has historically been more popular in the United States than in Ireland.

APRIL

'Twas the 18ᵗʰ of April in '75 (see poem The Midnight Ride of Paul Revere.) **Boston Marathon** is run near this date.

Good Friday commemorates the crucifixion of Jesus Christ by Pontius Pilate, believed by Christians to have taken place (traditionally) on April 1, 33 AD.

April 1: **April Fools's Day**

April 22: **Earth Day,** since 1970. (See Earthday.net)

Wednesday of the last full week of April —that is, the Wednesday before the last Saturday in April: **Administrative Assistants' Day**, which once upon a time was Secretaries' Day

Often the last Friday in April: **Arbor Day**, since 1872, but since planting conditions vary, it may occur from September to May; consult the National Arbor Day Foundation's list for Arbor Day Dates.

MAY

May 1: **May Day** refers to any of several public holidays. May Day is a "cross-quarter day," meaning that it falls approximately halfway between an equinox and a solstice.

The first Saturday in May: **Derby Day:** The running of the **Kentucky Derby** at Churchill Downs; the first of three horse races, the Triple Crown.

Second Sunday : **Mother's Day**

Third Saturday of May: **The Preakness, the second part of the Triple Crown,** at Pimlico, Baltimore, MD.

Third Saturday in May: **Armed Forces Day**

Last Monday in May since 1971: **Memorial Day**; from 1868 to 1970 it was celebrated on May 30 and was called Decoration Day.

May 5: **Cinco de Maya (Latin American festival for the 5ᵗʰ of May).** It is primarily a celebration of Mexican culture by Mexican-Americans living in the United States. Although this is the anniversary of the victory of the Mexican Army over the French at the Battle of Puebla in 1862, Cinco de Mayo is far more important in the USA than in México itself. Additionally, this "holiday" is often mistaken by Americans as being Mexican Independence Day, which is actually observed on September 16.

JUNE

Second Saturday in June: **The Belmont Stakes–the third part of the Triple Crown,** is run the at Belmont Park, NY.

June 14th: **Flag Day**

June 19: **Juneteenth**-primarily an African-American holiday honoring the end of slavery in the United States.

Third Sunday in June: **Fathers' Day**

JULY

July 4: **Independence Day**

SEPTEMBER

First Monday in September: **Labor Day**

September or October: **Rosh Hashanah** depending on Hebrew calendar; traditional beginning of the Jewish High Holidays and celebration of the start of a new year on the Hebrew calendar. **Yom Kippur:** Traditional end of the highest of the Jewish High Holidays.

OCTOBER

Second Monday in October: **Columbus Day**—federal holiday since 1971

October 24: **United Nations Day**

October 31: **Halloween**. Celebrates All Hallow's Eve. Children go trick-or-treating to neighbors who give away some sort of treat. Not generally observed by businesses.

NOVEMBER

Tuesday on or after November 2: **Election Day**

November whenever: Sadie Hawkins Day, when women ask men for dates, usually to a dance or other social event, breaking with tradition. Named for the character "Sadie Hawkins" from the long-running comic strip *Li'l Abner*.

November 11th: **Veterans Day** (except from 1971 to 1977, inclusive, when it was celebrated on the fourth Monday in October; formerly known as Armistice). A traditional observation is a moment of silence at 11 AM remembering those who fought for peace. (Commemorates the cease-fire in the 1918 armistice which was scheduled for "the eleventh hour of the eleventh day of the eleventh month."

Fourth Thursday in November: **Thanksgiving** , starts the *holiday season* in the winter, traditionally running between Thanksgiving and New Year's Day, which encompasses the **Winter solstice, Christmas, Hanukkah, and Kwanzaa.**

DECEMBER

December 25th: **Christmas**, a Christian holiday and a federal holiday:

MORE VOCABULARY

Large Size Vocabularies: You can download PDFs with the full body of information about these large sizes (1) behemoth, colossal, colossus, and cyclopian (2) gargantuan, gigantic, goliath (3) jumbo, leviathan, mammoth, massive, titanic, along with teachers' guides containing explanations and quiz answers from: http://www.wordwebvocabulary.com/bonus/Large_sizes_free_bonus_1.pdf

Or you can order hard copies of *Large, Larger, Larger*, a booklet which I describe as, "*An entertaining, educational, edifying experience and an enlightening exercise in advanced literacy for middle- and high-school students that incorporates reading, writing, mathematical computation, research, reporting and art*" from http://www.seepub.com. Click on education materials.

SAGE EDUCATION ENTERPRISES' PRODUCTS
http://www.seepub.com/educational.html

Writing and Reciting CHALLENGES for every classroom
How to Structure an Interdisciplinary Curriculum
Vocabulary: The Vehicle to the Art of Seeing
Science Vocabulary
Social Studies Vocabulary
Interdisciplinary Guide to Ancient Egypt including notes on the opera Aida
Interdisciplinary Guide to Ancient Greece
Interdisciplinary Guide to Medieval / Middle Ages
Interdisciplinary Guide to the Vikings

Manufactured By: RR Donnelley
                    Momence, IL USA
                    June , 2010